INVEST MY WAY

INVEST MY WAY

MAKING MONEY WITH BLUE CHIP SHARES ON THE AUSTRALIAN STOCK MARKET

ALAN HULL

Wrightbooks

First published in 2012 by Wrightbooks
an imprint of John Wiley & Sons Australia, Ltd
42 McDougall St, Milton Qld 4064

Office also in Melbourne

Typeset in ITC Berkeley Oldstyle Std Book 11/14

© Alan Hull 2012

The moral rights of the author have been asserted

National Library of Australia Cataloguing-in-Publication data:

Author:	Hull, Alan, 1962-
Title:	Invest my way: making money with blue chip shares on the Australian stock market / Alan Hull.
ISBN:	9781118319314 (pbk.)
Notes:	Includes index.
Subjects:	Blue-chip stocks. Investments. Finance, personal–Australia.
Dewey Number:	332.6322

Cover design by Peter Reardon, Pipeline Design <www.pipelinedesign.com.au>

Back cover image: used courtesy of Sky News

Microsoft Word, Microsoft Excel and Microsoft Paint screenshots used with permission from Microsoft.

Adobe product screenshots reprinted with permission from Adobe Systems Incorporated.

Printed in Australia by Ligare Book Printer

10 9 8 7 6 5 4 3 2

Disclaimer
The material in this publication is of the nature of general comment only, and neither purports nor intends to be advice. Readers should not act on the basis of any matter in this publication without considering (and if appropriate, taking) professional advice with due regard to their own particular circumstances. The author and publisher expressly disclaim all and any liability to any person, whether a purchaser of this publication or not, in respect of anything and of the consequences of anything done or omitted to be done by any such person in reliance, whether whole or partial, upon the whole or any part of the contents of this publication.

To my soul mate, Debra

Contents

Acknowledgements

I am the sum total of those around me—both now and before me.

Simon Sherwood—whose support and help made this book possible.

Martin Roth—a man for whom I and many others in my industry have a deep respect.

The management and staff of Lincoln Indicators—my sincerest thanks for producing such a wonderful product and being so agreeable to all my requests.

Kathryn and Matthew, my little mates—you stop me from taking myself too seriously.

My readers—if you keep reading, I'll keep writing.

About the author

A second-generation share trader and investor, Alan Hull owned his first share when he was just eight years old. As a result of his early start in the stock market, most of the lessons that the average investor will learn during their adult life were second nature to Alan by the time he was in his twenties.

Alan has also had a keen interest in mathematics from a very young age and was an IT expert from the early days of personal computing. Employing this combination of skills and his experience over the past two to three decades as a modern share trader and investor has transformed Alan into one of Australia's leading stock market experts.

Alan is highly respected within the Australian investment industry, regularly writing articles and presenting for the Australian Securities Exchange, the Australian Technical Analysts Association, the Australian Investors Association and the Trading and Investing Expo.

Apart from writing his own best-selling books, he has also contributed to other publications, including Martin Roth's best-selling *Top Stocks* series; Daryl Guppy's international book, *Better Stock Trading*; Jim Berg's series, *Shares to Buy and When*; and *The Wiley Trading Guide*.

Rather than being content as a private investor, author and educator, Alan is also a licensed financial adviser. In recent years he has successfully managed millions of dollars of other people's money, consistently beating all the major ASX market averages.

One of Alan's most notable decisions as a fund manager was to move all his holdings to cash in the latter half of 2007 and not reinvest in shares until mid 2009, preserving his clients' capital throughout one of the worst financial crises of recent times.

With a focus on the practical, Alan covers all the bases in this comprehensive guide on investing in Australian blue chip shares. Like his other books, *Invest My Way* is compulsory reading for anyone who hopes to make consistent profits from buying and selling Australian shares.

Preface

My primary area of expertise is investing in blue chip shares. I began my career in the stock market at the ripe old age of eight, when my father bought me my first share. This initial encounter with the stock market proved fruitful and I've been hooked ever since. I love buying and selling shares and everything related to the stock market. I've never forgotten the feeling I had when I sold my first share for a profit and thought, 'Wow, this is money for jam'.

I started out by trying to invest like my father—big mistake. He's one of these unique animals who gets away with having a totally discretionary approach to investing. He loves doing his own research and spends literally thousands of hours at it. He sends company secretaries around the twist by pumping them with never-ending requests for information; he devours daily, weekly and monthly newspapers and periodicals; and he is constantly studying assay results, annual reports, profit and loss sheets, and the like.

To give you some idea of his discretionary ability, he foresaw the 1987 stock market crash and, as a result, he sold all his shares in September of 1987 and completely sidestepped the carnage (see figure 1, overleaf).

Anyway, initially I tried the same approach, but because I didn't have his appetite for doing the research I cut corners and, as a direct consequence, the stock market cut into my bank balance. Bottom line: if you don't have a real interest in what you're doing then don't do it. A lot of people are in love with the *idea* of taking money from the market, but at the end of the day you have to have a passion for the process, not just the proceeds.

Figure 1: the All Ordinaries index from September 1986, showing the extent of the crash in October 1987

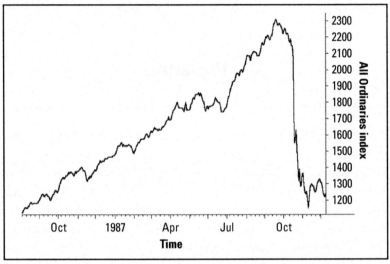

Source: SuperCharts version 4 by Omega Research © 1997.

Furthermore, Dad was into small capitalisation mining shares and so, as a result, I was too. In the early days it was easy come and easy go—especially the go bit. My problem was that I never wanted to accept that the music had stopped, and I would hang on to a deteriorating position until it had well and truly turned into a loss. Then I would do something really clever like averaging down by buying more shares at a lower price—only to realise further down the track that all I'd done was compounded the original loss. Really clever stuff!

But somewhere around the traps (I probably read it in an American book) I heard that blue chip shares were the elephants of the stock market—slowly plodding along in a nice predictable manner, not giving their owners any sudden surprises. So I started investing in blue chip shares—where I lost money more slowly. Ideally, blue chip investors target growth opportunities, such as Cochlear was in the late 1990s through to the start of the new millennium (see figure 2).

Figure 2: Cochlear is the type of share that I'm aiming for—plodding slowly upwards

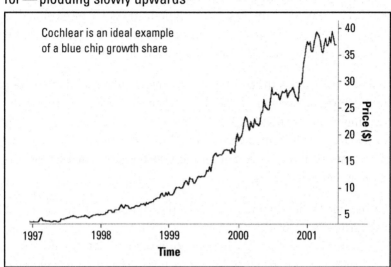

Cochlear is an ideal example of a blue chip growth share

Source: SuperCharts version 4 by Omega Research © 1997.

While this all sounds a bit humorous, it did give me the breathing space to learn my craft, because I now had sustainability on my side. The stock market will teach us how to invest through our hip-pocket nerves, if we just have the ability to hang in there long enough to learn the lessons. The trouble for the vast majority of newcomers to the market is that they just don't stick it out for long enough.

Anyway, I spent many years, starting from the late 1980s, trying every approach to stock market investing and trading imaginable. I tried to ride on the coat-tails of prominent market experts like the Kerry Packers of this world. To cut a long story short I discovered that Kerry was a very slippery character and one that defied mimicking—not unlike his offshore nemesis, Sir Rupert Murdoch.

I hunted for arbitrage trading opportunities—situations where a trader can capitalise on price inconsistencies across different markets. For instance, BHP Billiton trades on both the Australian and London stock exchanges simultaneously and from time to time it may offer up an opportunity through price deviations across these two independent markets. Of course, this type of trading tactic is far more suited to large institutions that have the sort of big fat purses needed to really make this type of marginal trading opportunity pay off.

I tried to piggyback the overnight movements in the US stock market by buying first thing in the morning when the US market took a dip overnight, and then selling out when the US markets recovered a day or two later. It all seemed very logical, but given the results I achieved it became painfully apparent to me that the stock market isn't an entirely rational animal.

Then there's the rumour mill: buy the rumour, sell the fact. But ask anyone who paid $1 a share for Crown Casino back in the late 1990s just before Kerry Packer bought it out for a lot less and they'll confirm that it doesn't always work that way. The rumour mill works just great if you're receiving accurate and timely intelligence but, as you'll discover for yourself if you try, most of the time you're the patsy buying up the stock from the people who started the rumour!

So, as you can see, I've pretty much covered the entire spectrum when it comes to buying and selling shares. Alas, it was to be many years and tens of thousands of dollars lost before I found my groove in the marketplace — investing in blue chip shares. I am both a trader and an investor in blue chip shares. As you will discover later on in this book, a trader is simply an investor who invests in growth stocks as opposed to an investor who buys and holds income stocks.

Of course, in order to provide a truly complete guide on how to invest in blue chip shares, I have covered both of these primary approaches. They each have a section of this book all to themselves, as they are essentially mutually exclusive methodologies, but where they do intersect is in overall market timing. This is because there's a time to buy and sell growth stocks, and a different time to acquire income stocks.

So another section of this book deals exclusively with market timing, and I dispel the notion that it's 'time in the market, not market timing that counts'. The simple fact is that success in the market requires a measure of both philosophies. And as this material starts to get into a rather tertiary discussion and requires the reader to have a few basic concepts in hand to fully appreciate it, I have put this section last.

Thus the discussion of 'Financial markets as complex adaptive systems' (chapter 12) appears near the end of this book, and we will start at the beginning with the more fundamental issues of 'What is an investor?' (chapter 1) and 'Managing financial products' (chapter 2). So in the first section we will lay the groundwork for what's to come by addressing the more general concepts that all investors should know.

I will be utilising both the stock market and the property market to illustrate these key concepts. You will discover that while we're dealing in different forms of financial products, there are a very large number of parallels between stock market and property investors. For starters we're all in the *business* of making money.

At every opportunity I have used working examples to illustrate ideas and concepts because I believe this is the best way to teach. Wherever possible, rocket science (read: maths) has been kept to an absolute minimum, but it is obviously unavoidable in some instances. I recommend that you read through the chapters chronologically, as the content has been presented in an order that puts each new piece of information into context to make it easier to understand and retain.

I am often asked why I sacrifice the time and effort to write books if I am so successful at investing in the stock market. The reason is that it's not just about money: writing books is about sharing my knowledge with others. And by passing my knowledge on to others I greatly amplify its worth, hopefully improve the quality of other people's lives to some degree and reinforce my own understanding by having to write everything down. Thus I hope you learn as much from *Invest My Way* as I have learnt from writing it.

Alan Hull

June 2012

PART I

*The business
of investing in blue
chip shares*

Chapter 1
What is an investor?

I always like to start any discussion by defining terms, just to make sure we're all on the same page (excuse the pun). So let's start with a succinct definition of the word *invest*, taken directly from the fourth edition of the Australian Concise Oxford Dictionary: *Apply or use money for profit.*

That sounds simple enough, but to really understand the full impact of this statement we need to answer some other questions first and, while they may seem completely unrelated, I would suggest they are not.

- What is a worker?
- What is a manager?

These seem like simple enough questions, but if we probe beyond the brief and obvious answers, we will uncover some very interesting definitions and distinctions.

Worker

Put very simply, a worker is someone who works for someone else in exchange for money. But if we want to be a little more precise about this apparently straightforward function, then we could also say that a worker is someone who sells his or her time for money, and that time includes both that person's labour and expertise. A typical working situation would be an individual who spends 40 hours per week working for someone else in exchange for approximately $65 000 per year. This is a typical situation, given that these parameters are based on the current Australian averages for hours in a working week and annual wages.

The average person will spend about 40 years of his or her life (from the age of 20 to age 60) working for someone else in order to finance their lifestyle and, hopefully, their retirement. For our purposes, we will define a worker as someone who is directly involved in the process of manufacturing a product or supplying a service. A self-employed person is someone who is a self-managed worker—that is, he or she both manages and is directly involved in the process of manufacturing a product or supplying a service. But if, for instance, someone oversees the production of goods but doesn't have to be directly involved in the production process itself, then he or she would fit into the next category—manager.

Manager

A manager is someone who controls a system or a process as opposed to being directly involved in the process itself. While it may be argued that a management role is in fact a form of work, and therefore a manager is a worker, for the purpose of this discussion we will define working and managing as two distinctly separate functions or roles. For example, although managing my investments does take time and some degree of effort, it would be inaccurate and somewhat misleading to say that I'm working my investments.

Investor

Now that we've clarified the difference between these two functions, let's apply this understanding to acquiring money. In the first instance we have the worker who sells his or her time for income; this is the most common and conventional way for any of us to acquire money and unfortunately very few of us go beyond this simple method of feeding and clothing ourselves.

But the few of us who do, see ourselves as managers where we control systems or processes that generate money—we are businesspeople. Harking back to the example of my investments, I manage (as opposed to work) my portfolio of blue chip shares, which takes about 20 minutes per week. Or, to put it another way, someone who manages a system or process that generates money is said to be *making* money as opposed to a worker who sells their time to someone else to *earn* money.

Now we come to the meat of the matter, because any business that utilises financial products, such as shares and property, is said to be an investment business. And finally, anyone who manages an investment business is an investor and they are *applying or using money for profit*.

While this explanation of what an investor is may all seem very longwinded, it is of the utmost importance that investors see themselves as businesspeople if they want to be successful.

And now we need to differentiate between investors who manage their own affairs and those who have others manage their money—and it's all a question of control.

Control

Unfortunately the average individual assumes that others have the expertise and resources that they don't—a common and erroneous assumption (also one that the investment industry loves to feed on through clever advertising). Although many people do lack the necessary knowledge, it can be easily acquired through books such as this one; you would be surprised at the vast array of resources available to the average do-it-yourself (DIY) investor.

It is often said and it is very true that no-one will take better care of your money than you will. I'll add to this: you can get someone else to make investment decisions for you, but ultimately the responsibility for your money stays with you. Advisers are paid to give advice (for which they are responsible), but you will find it very hard to hold them accountable for your money if anything goes wrong, such as the losses suffered by shareholders in the failure of the insurance behemoth HIH Insurance Limited.

But given that you're reading this book, I think it's a fairly safe assumption on my part that you are more willing than most to become a self-manager of your financial situation. And it may interest you to know that the reason for the current boom in DIY investment is because many self-managed DIY superannuation funds are reportedly doing far better than many managed investment vehicles.

There are several reasons for this: DIY investors aren't as restricted as fund managers when it comes to investment tactics; DIY funds don't attract many of the fees that the managed funds charge; and a DIY investor's sole motivation is the performance of the fund and, in the vast majority of cases, nothing else.

Fund managers

Of course at some point or through circumstances, we've all had to outsource the management of part if not all of our investment capital to a third party. Most commonly it's when we got our first job and we had to make contributions to a compulsory superannuation fund. So let's take a brief look at some of the key issues associated with employing someone else to manage your money.

If you've ever made enquiries about joining a managed fund then you were probably shown a glossy brochure containing a pie chart giving the breakdown for allocating capital to different investment media, such as 40 per cent to property, 50 per cent to Australian equities and 10 per cent to fixed deposits. These pie charts are often far more complex than this and will even delve into capital allocation per industry sector and residential property versus commercial property and so on.

But here's the silly bit: because they've disclosed these allocations to you when they signed you up to the fund, they are committed to them. Hence if the stock market goes into a sustained decline then your money will go into a sustained decline along with it. And many investors well know the pain of being exposed to shares during 2008, when the market lost nearly half its value.

This is why it's so important when someone else is managing your money to have regular interviews with your financial adviser so you can authorise any changes they need to make in the event of changes in the investment environment. Modern disclosure and compliance rules mean that fund managers can't necessarily take your money out of the market, even when that may be the best course of action.

Of course, as a DIY investor you can withdraw your money from the market, because you aren't subject to the same disclosure rules. The reason for this is quite simple, as the idea of disclosure to yourself would be a bit silly.

Anyway, having been directly involved in funds management myself, I can personally attest to the fact that the primary concern of many managed funds is not performance. This is partly due to the fact that the fees charged by most funds are directly proportional to the amount of capital under management as opposed to their performance, and partly due to the cost of meeting regulatory requirements.

Funds management companies will typically put their energies into attracting new money into their funds rather than into achieving the best possible performance, as it is usually the former that primarily determines their profitability. I do appreciate, however, that these two objectives aren't entirely mutually exclusive.

Then there are the administrative and compliance issues to deal with that, unfortunately, can have considerable sway over the design of an investment strategy. In other words, an investment strategy can be compromised (read: watered down) for the sake of streamlining the administration processes, minimising overheads and reducing or eliminating potential compliance issues.

As you can see, employing someone else to manage your money is actually a bit more of a minefield than most people would imagine. Suffice it to say that even when we employ others to manage our money for us, we are still stuck with the task of managing the managers. Consequently, whether we manage our own money or let others do it for us, it pays to have a good working knowledge of the business of investing and what we are investing in.

Self-management

So let's take a look at how easy it is to manage your own portfolio of blue chip shares using a very simple set of criteria. Now this simple set of criteria is designed to identify what is commonly referred to as growth stocks—these are shares that we would buy in the hope that the share price will rise over time and we will realise capital growth: hence the name growth stocks.

Our main criterion is this: we want to identify quality blue chip companies where the share price is trending up. This means that we want large capitalisation companies that are financially very sound—that is, blue chip companies—where the share price is already rising in value. More specifically, where the share price has already risen over the course of at least one year. This is a very important point because, if the share price is already rising, then the balance of probability suggests it will continue to do so. The chart in figure 1.1 is a typical example of the sort of price activity we're looking for.

Figure 1.1: example of a weekly price chart

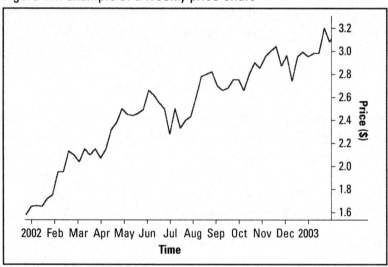

Source: MetaStock.

If this all sounds simple then that's because it is. The first thing I point out to anyone who wants to learn about the stock market is that it's not at all complicated, but that is in fact the problem. Most people won't hold with simple truths because they assume that success can only be achieved through complexity—otherwise everyone would be doing it, right? Wrong. First, most people won't take on the risk of failure and, second, success in most cases comes from having the discipline to stick with simple ideas that work.

I can give you the simple ideas that work, but dealing with the risk of failure and having self-discipline can only come from within ourselves. Hence it is not knowledge that is the elusive factor when it comes to success, but these other personal traits, or rather qualities, that unfortunately cannot be learned through reading books.

Proven results

It might provide some motivation if I show you what can be achieved using the simple criteria cited above. From July 2000 I began conducting a series of seminars where we applied these criteria to the Australian stock market to construct portfolios of about eight blue chip shares. The purpose of these seminars was to illustrate the effectiveness of this simple set of criteria in real time. Those who attended these seminars could monitor the performance for themselves during the coming year. Four portfolios were developed over a total period of four years and five months, from July 2000 to December 2004. Note that this period largely predates the recent boom. Tables 1.1 to 1.4 (overleaf) show the complete set of results.

Table 1.1: portfolio results, 2000–01

Share	Weight	Change	Status	Profit or loss
BKL	12.5%	3.45%	Sold	0.43%
IDT	12.5%	–30.42%	Sold	–3.80%
COH	12.5%	–4.38%	Sold	–0.55%
TOL	12.5%	162.30%	Open	20.29%
SGN	12.5%	61.27%	Sold	7.66%
LAC	12.5%	27.09%	Sold	3.39%
CPU	12.5%	7.37%	Sold	0.92%
FLT	12.5%	35.12%	Sold	4.39%
All Ords ⇨ down 5.44%			**Total profit = 32.73%**	

Table 1.2: portfolio results, 2001–02

Share	Weight	Change	Status	Profit or loss
COH	11.11%	−2.49%	Sold	−0.28%
NFD	11.11%	45.34%	Open	5.04%
SFL	11.11%	60.00%	Sold	6.67%
BRS	11.11%	7.35%	Sold	0.82%
GLD	11.11%	35.87%	Sold	3.99%
WSF	11.11%	−4.61%	Sold	−0.51%
TOL	11.11%	8.87%	Sold	0.99%
WES	11.11%	3.64%	Sold	0.40%
MIG	11.11%	−0.36%	Sold	−0.04%
All Ords ⇨ down 4.69%			**Total profit = 17.08%**	

Table 1.3: portfolio results, 2002–03

Share	Weight	Change	Status	Profit or loss
ALN	20%	48.93%	Open	9.79%
ANN	15%	−22.48%	Sold	−3.37%
GNS	10%	53.46%	Open	5.35%
SHV	20%	50.60%	Open	10.12%
AVJ	10%	101.04%	Open	10.10%
FKP	10%	84.56%	Open	8.46%
BRS	10%	37.74%	Open	3.77%
FFL	5%	8.25%	Open	0.41%
All Ords ⇨ up 10.12%			**Total profit = 44.63%**	

Table 1.4: portfolio results, 2003–04

Share	Weight	Change	Status	Profit or loss
RUP	15%	47.46%	Open	7.12%
GUD	15%	60.37%	Sold	9.06%
FAN	9%	49.85%	Sold	4.49%
FBU	9%	−3.87%	Sold	−0.35%
FWD	10%	51.28%	Sold	5.13%
SMS	15%	8.69%	Sold	1.30%
AVJ	12%	4.79%	Sold	0.57%
UTB	15%	0.79%	Sold	0.12%
All Ords ⇨ up 24.13%			**Total profit = 27.44%**	

You will see in the Status column that some of the shares were sold before the end of their respective simulations. This is because they breached a predetermined stop loss limit and were therefore automatically eliminated from the portfolio. Interestingly, the use of stop losses is considered an essential practice by most DIY investors when managing a growth portfolio, but is not a practice widely used by modern fund managers.

Business skills

The results shown in tables 1.1 to 1.4 are testimony to what can be achieved using a very simple approach that requires very little time and effort. But this simple approach, which will be elaborated on at greater length in later chapters, is only part of the total skill set needed for achieving success in designing and running our own investment business.

As you can see, we can take the view that we're in business for ourselves whether we have a job, are self-employed or even retired and just managing our investments. And seeing ourselves as businesspeople gives us the ability to steer ourselves towards a financial destiny of our own choosing—if we possess the appropriate skills.

Charting

And speaking of the appropriate skills, I find that while most people who are even just a little bit curious about the stock market possess a rudimentary knowledge of fundamental analysis (the interpretation of financial data), there are quite a few who have virtually no knowledge of technical analysis. Technical analysis is simply the study of price charts (as opposed to financial data), and having a basic understanding of both forms of analysis is almost essential in this modern technological age of investing. So before moving on, I thought this would be a good juncture to quickly cover the basics of technical analysis, colloquially known as charting.

What we are looking at when we study a price chart is the change in price over a given period of time. Hence the vertical scale on any price chart is the price of the instrument in question, while the horizontal scale is time.

The line-on-close chart of BHP Billiton in figure 1.2 showing slightly more than 12 months of weekly price activity is a typical example of the sort of chart you would see in a newspaper or magazine. This chart would technically be referred to as a weekly line-on-close chart, and it is created by drawing a line connecting the weekly closing prices of BHP Billiton (BHP) during the period shown. I've used this type of chart already in this book—it is the simplest form of price chart available.

Figure 1.2: BHP Billiton—line-on-close chart

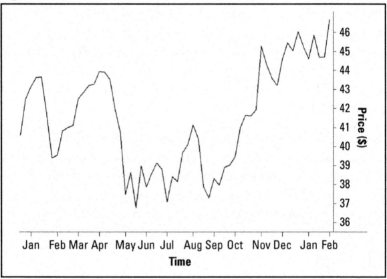

Source: MetaStock.

The closing price is considered to be the most important piece of price information, but there is more to the story than just the closing price. There are in fact four individual bits of price information to consider and they are:

- open—the price the market initially trades at when it first opens

- high—the highest price the market trades at during the trading period

- low—the lowest price the market trades at during the trading period

- close—the last price the market trades at just before the market closes.

Note the use of the word *market* in the previous explanation; in this context I am using it in its generic form. In other words, I may describe the buying and selling of any individual share or financial instrument, such as BHP Billiton, as a market, or I may use it to describe the stock market as a whole. Whichever the case, it should be reasonably obvious what I mean from the context in which I am applying it.

Furthermore, as a form of shorthand, I may identify a specific share, such as BHP Billiton, by just its share code and not its full name. Usually I will use the company's full name initially but then refer to it by its share code from that point on. Anyway, let's get back to our discussion on price charts.

OHLC bar charts

Probably the simplest way in which to display all four bits of price information is with the aid of the OHLC bar chart (see figure 1.3). OHLC is shorthand for open, high, low and close.

Figure 1.3: BHP Billiton — OHLC bar chart, where each bar represents a single trading period

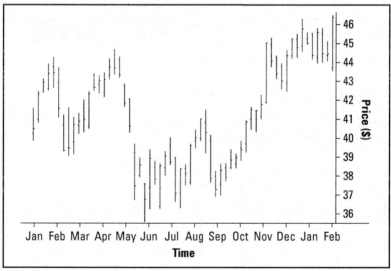

Source: MetaStock.

In figure 1.3 each trading period (a week) is represented by a bar that has a tick to the left of the bar and another tick to the right. The top of the bar and the bottom of the bar represent the price range of a given trading period (that is, the high and the low), while the tick to the left of the bar is the opening price and the tick to the right represents the closing price. That's all fairly straightforward, and probably the simplest way of displaying all four bits of price information.

Candlestick charts

Now let's move on to the type of chart that's my personal favourite: the candlestick chart. It also conveys all four bits of price information, and while it is the type of chart that I'll be using later on in this book, you will also see the other chart types from time to time. Hopefully this will help you to familiarise yourself with all these different types of price charts.

Anyway, candlestick charts are a little more complex than the chart types we've looked at to this point and so they warrant a slightly more detailed explanation. Candlestick charts are so called because they use a single candle for each trading period. The larger section of each candle is called the 'real body', whereas the thin parts on the top or bottom are called 'shadows'.

Candlestick charts originated in Japan and have been in use for several centuries. There is a vast body of material on how to interpret these charts, including a wide variety of names for the different shapes of candles that can occur (see figure 1.4).

Figure 1.4: elements of a candlestick chart

white candle

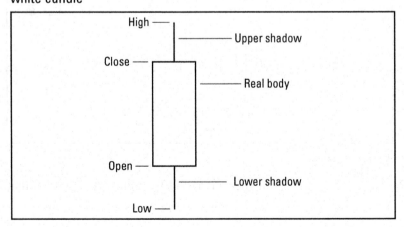

black candle

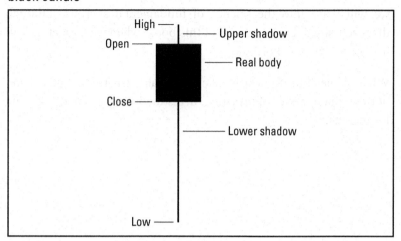

Let's go back to our 12-month chart of BHP, but this time let's use candlesticks. Compare figure 1.5 with figure 1.3 (the OHLC chart of BHP, on p. 13) and you can see how it provides a far more meaningful visual impression than the OHLC chart does.

Figure 1.5: BHP Billiton — candlestick chart

Source: MetaStock.

So we've now covered the basics of charting and, when appropriate, we will delve into the science of fundamental analysis, although that's actually not until part III of this book, when we look at how to manage an income portfolio.

What we need to do next is take a look at the nature of shares and our two main modes of investing: investing for growth and investing for income.

Chapter 2

Managing financial products

Now I haven't forgotten that this is a book about blue chip shares, but while we're exploring these more preliminary concepts about investing, there is no reason why our discussion can't also include property. What's more, I'm sure there are many readers who may already have had exposure as investors to the property market and so will find the analogies and examples relating to the property market very helpful.

This chapter also includes a detailed discussion of risk, and will introduce you to the 2 per cent risk-management rule. I'm pointing this out because, in the previous chapter, I said that it is common practice to manage growth shares using some form of stop loss strategy, which tells us when to sell. Well, the 2 per cent risk rule works hand in hand with our stop loss strategy to regulate our market exposure. It is also critical to success when managing growth stocks. So it will literally pay you to read this bit carefully.

The investment business

Investing in shares and property is undoubtedly a business activity, given that you both own and manage the process, but you don't have to work *in* the process—we all make money from our investments, even when we're not there to watch them. The money we make from shares and property is derived in two ways: capital growth on the value of the asset itself, and income from the asset, such as rent from a tenant or an annual dividend payment from shares that we hold. Figure 2.1 shows what this investment business model would look like, in very general terms.

Figure 2.1: business model for Investments Pty Ltd

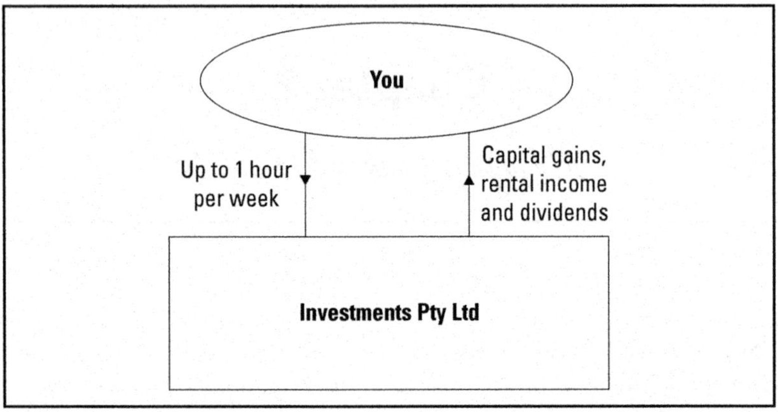

Investing

The greatest single area of confusion for most would-be investors is understanding the difference between *investing* in shares or property, and *trading* in shares or property. As already discussed, the word *invest* means to apply or use money for profit, which includes any money-making endeavour that requires money. So to describe yourself as an investor could mean that you've had to spend money to be self-employed (which is virtually the case for all self-employed people), you're a property or share investor, or you're even a worker who pays for your own uniform. Hence the tag 'investor' is not a very precise term, but one that manages to create a considerable degree of confusion.

Trading shares

The word *trade* means *buying and selling for profit*, which does make for a clear definition. If I say I am a share trader then I am stating that

I buy and sell shares for a profit, which sounds ridiculously simple, but there are deeper implications to this statement. For instance, if I am buying shares with the intention of selling them at a future date for a profit, then I would have to be expecting them to rise in value. And, as I've already stated, the funds management industry refers to this type of share as a growth stock because, hopefully, the share price will grow over time.

Share traders qualify as a type of investor because they are applying money to the stock market in order to generate a profit. Contrary to popular belief, people who deal in shares are not defined as traders by the number of trades they perform each year. This definition was created by a certain government department, and while it may serve its purposes well, it is very misleading for the rest of us. If you purchase a share with the intention of selling it for a profit at any time in the future, then you are a share trader. The value of the share must go up over time and you could sell it after one week, one year, 10 years or even longer.

Shares as assets

On the other hand, you can own shares as an investor and not be deemed a trader if you regard them as an income-producing asset—which is exactly how renowned investor Warren Buffett sees them. Warren Buffett's company, Berkshire Hathaway, is an asset-management company that buys interests in companies that are undervalued, improves their operation over time and then derives a very cost-effective income from them. Warren Buffett's favourite holding time is forever, because he buys interests in companies in order to derive an ongoing income from them rather than to sell them for profit.

In other words, he's primarily interested in the profits the company he invests in makes each year, and he views any capital growth as a bonus. And, unlike a share trader, who will sell shares that start to fall in value, Buffett will buy more shares because they represent a cheaper income stream. So a share trader wants to buy a rising share price and an investor (read: asset manager) wants to buy a high-income yield that occurs when the share price falls—perfectly opposed objectives!

Let's assume that a company pays an annual dividend of $1.00 and the share price is $10.00. (Hence the dividend yield or income yield = $1.00 ÷ $10.00 = 10 per cent per year.)

Now let's assume the share price drops to $8.00, but the dividend remains at $1.00 per annum—a not unlikely occurrence given that a company's profitability isn't necessarily linked to its share price. Therefore, the dividend yield would increase to $1.00 ÷ $8.00 = 12.5 per cent per year.

So if you want to buy a high-yielding stock, referred to by the funds management industry as an income stock, then the direction of the share price is largely irrelevant because, like Buffett, you have no intention of selling the shares at a later date. In fact, if the share price were to halve during a stock market crash, you would buy more shares because the yield will have doubled. This is where dollar cost averaging is used very effectively: you keep buying more shares as the share price drops and the dividend yield keeps rising, thus averaging up your income. Dollar cost averaging is therefore a very effective technique for investors like Warren Buffett.

So we have investors who are seeking growth, and investors who are seeking income. Putting it another way, we have traders and investors. I could differentiate using the terms *growth investors* and *income investors*, but given those are rather clumsy terms, I'll refer to them as traders and investors, where traders are growth investors and, unless otherwise stated, investors are income investors.

Trading or investing in property

Now let's turn our attention to real estate investment and look at how property can be either bought and sold for a profit, or held as an income-producing asset, just like shares. I'll use a real-world example here because recent developments in the property market will prove very illustrative. As many property investors are aware, there is a large population of baby boomers who are just around the corner from retirement. It has been broadly assumed that the members of this demographic group are shortly going to sell their family homes once the children have left, and retire en masse to locations more suited to a leisurely lifestyle than the suburbs: hence the massive investment in, and development of, inner-city apartments that we've seen in Australia since the turn of the millennium.

Now assume for a moment that you're an investor who owns an inner-city dwelling and you have to make a command decision as to whether you should retain the property for the rental income or sell it outright for a profit (read: capital growth). Given the expected migration of the baby boomers to the city, we know that if we sell into the resulting demand, then we can reasonably expect to make a good profit on the sale.

But what are our prospects if we want to retain the property indefinitely for the income stream? Not too good, I expect, because the baby boomers who are heading for the big smoke are going to be seriously cashed up, having sold the family home, and looking to buy their own apartments rather than pay rent to someone else. So given this particular scenario it would be my opinion that trading the apartment for a quick profit will probably prove more prudent than holding it for the long term as an income-producing asset. What's more, this opinion is supported by the general stagnation in inner-city apartment prices (around the time of writing).

Trading versus investing

Given the opposing perspectives of traders and investors, you can appreciate the importance of knowing which category you belong to. I frequently see share traders (investors seeking growth), applying Warren Buffett–style tactics to the stock market only to become totally confused when they don't achieve their intended profitable outcomes. There is also no one preferred path to take here, as there are many pros and cons to both trading and investing, as well as dealing in property or shares. In practice, most seasoned investors tend to have a degree of exposure to both modes of investing and both financial products, property and shares.

Shares are an intangible financial product, which makes them ideal to trade because they don't require any infrastructure. We don't have to physically take possession of the shares we buy, they don't require maintenance, and there is always a ready market of buyers and sellers. So all it takes for me to be a share trader is to have ready access to the stock market, which can be by phone to a stockbroker or via the internet.

Property, on the other hand, is typically very stable in terms of its income revenue, and the banks are far friendlier when it comes to lending money to finance a property portfolio than they are to financing a share portfolio. But buying and selling the family home is enough of a saga, in my opinion, without making a business out of it by actually trading in properties — imagine the headaches. Hence, while there is the odd exception, such as buying and selling inner-city apartments for capital growth, my approach to property investment leans towards being an income investor with a very, very long-term outlook.

Risk

Now that we've clarified the difference between trading and investing, we can move on to the next area of general confusion, and that is the concept of risk. We'll start with a definition:

> *Risk is the product of the possibility of incurring a loss, and the potential magnitude of the loss.*

In other words, the risk of dying in a car accident is the probability of being in a car accident multiplied by the probability of dying in a car accident. Therefore, if your chances of being in a car accident were 1 in 100 and the probability of dying in a car accident were 1 in 1000 car accidents, then the probability of dying in a car accident would be one in 100 000. Volvo, for example, which is renowned for automotive safety, reduces your chances of dying in a car accident by downwardly adjusting 'the magnitude of the loss' in this quantitative definition through the provision of airbags, crumple zones and similar devices. Of course the first part of the equation — the possibility of being in a car accident — is largely up to us, as drivers, to minimise.

It's worth noting that there is risk in everything we do and so there is no such thing as no risk. It is absolutely true that we could die crossing the road some time tomorrow, and we would very likely avoid being worse off if we didn't get out of bed—because the possibility of incurring a loss would probably be greatly reduced as a result. Often we either don't realise that there's a chance of something going wrong, or we don't recognise that there is anything at stake; that is, we assume there is nothing to lose. But the most common problem I encounter when dealing with investors is the exact opposite—they irrationally assume there is a high probability of incurring a massive loss.

Perceived risk

Humankind's greatest fear is of the unknown, because if we can't quantify the risk then our imaginations take over and we fear the worst. Stock markets around the world dropped dramatically in the lead-up to the first Gulf War, only to recover just as rapidly once the actual hostilities broke out—bad news is better than no news. This can be seen in figure 2.2, which shows the Dow Jones Industrial Average index, which dropped just on 20 per cent before bouncing all the way back up.

Figure 2.2: Dow Jones index, May 1990–July 1991

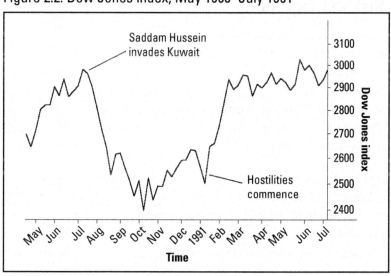

Source: MetaStock.

If we can't measure the risk or we don't understand the risk, then we can only perceive the risk, and this is a qualitative form of analysis. Qualitative risk is ruled by our emotions and imagination, and is largely erroneous, as some university researchers have discovered through their investigations of the human state of worry. By measuring the actual outcomes of things we worry about, they determined that only 2 per cent of what we worry about actually comes to pass.

But erroneous or not, perceived risk has the power to either prevent us from taking action at all or, more commonly, to impede our ability to act objectively. Therefore, we need to eliminate this form of risk, and the best way to do this is with knowledge. If we fear the unknown then the best course of action is to eliminate it through education. For example, I was an electronics technician in a former life and so I wouldn't hesitate to pull the back off a television set or any other electrical appliance. But the thought of cooking a dinner party for friends fills me with dread because of my limited knowledge of cooking—I would definitely risk looking very stupid.

Risk management

I could easily eliminate this perceived risk by taking cooking lessons and acquiring the relevant knowledge and skills. Many investors also perceive imaginary risks that they consider to be beyond their control, because they have never been exposed to the science of risk management. Risk management is the assessment and control of risk. The best way to explain how risk management works is by using a real-world example.

Let's assume we're playing a game of coin toss where the probability of losing each game is 50 per cent. In other words, it's a fair game of chance where the odds of getting a head or a tail are even. If we play 100 games of coin toss then we can create a chart showing the balance of outcomes for 100 consecutive tosses of a coin, as shown in figure 2.3.

Figure 2.3: results for 100 coin tosses

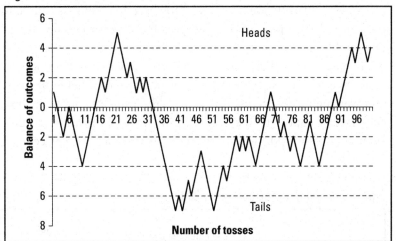

Although tossing a coin 100 times is certainly not a scientifically conclusive exercise, it will serve our purpose, which is to measure the maximum possible loss we face when tossing a coin. We know the balance of outcomes for a fair game of chance will always return to zero because the outcomes are even and, in figure 2.3, we can see that if we were betting on heads the greatest loss we could expect to encounter is to be seven tosses down. Therefore, the probable outcome of this game is to break even, while we risk suffering a maximum loss of seven tosses.

Controlling risk

This is the easy bit. If we were wagering $1 on each toss of the coin, then to control our risk we would simply need to make sure we had at least $8 to play with at the start (one more than seven because you need at least $1 in your possession in order to keep playing). This would ensure our survival and we'd live long enough to enjoy the outcome of breaking even — not much to look forward to, really. But fortunately for us the stock market offers a much better outcome.

Share trading

This is the good bit. Given that the All Ordinaries index (All Ords), which is the Australian stock market index, has risen 9 per cent per year (non-compounding) on average for the past 100 years, the outcome from your average blue chip share portfolio should be in the ballpark of 9 per cent capital growth per year plus the average annual dividend yield of the index. Of course, you should note that while past performance is our best guide in most instances, it is no guarantee of future performance—a point rightly made in many an investment prospectus. But, as with the game of coin toss, share traders can expect to incur significant losses from time to time, such as during 2002 when the All Ords dropped 11 per cent, as figure 2.4 shows.

Figure 2.4: All Ordinaries index, 2002

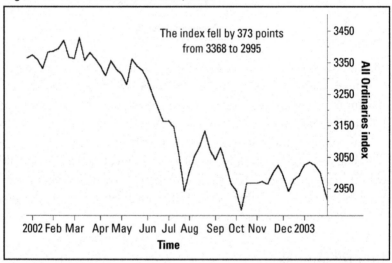

Source: MetaStock.

So while our frame of reference in the stock market is 9 per cent per year in our favour over the long term, we need to make sure we can survive long enough to enjoy it. Hence, in order to control the risks involved in share trading, we need a way of ensuring our sustainability. This is achieved by regulating the size of our losses.

First, let's assume we are going to start trading shares with a total capital of $50 000 (the value of our growth portfolio plus any cash reserves) and we will lose $5000 on each share we trade. So after 10 consecutive losing trades we would be wiped out—not a very nice prospect. Now consider a slight variation on this theme, where we risk only 10 per cent of our current total capital. Table 2.1 shows how our losses would become smaller with each losing trade. Note that once again we are starting with shares and cash worth a total of $50000.

Table 2.1: losses if we only risk 10 per cent of total capital

Loss	Amount lost	Total capital after loss
1	$5000.00	$45000.00
2	$4500.00	$40500.00
3	$4050.00	$36450.00
4	$3645.00	$32805.00
5	$3280.50	$29524.50
6	$2952.45	$26572.05
7	$2657.20	$23914.84
8	$2391.48	$21523.36

This method of regulating our losses will increase our sustainability considerably, more than doubling the number of losses it would take to wipe us out. In fact, if we were to call it quits once we had reduced our initial bank of $50000 down to $5000, then we could sustain up to 23 consecutive losses. This deterioration of $50000 can be seen graphically in figure 2.5, which compares an equity curve (a graph showing the value of a trading account) based on a 10 per cent reducing loss with an equity curve based on a 2 per cent reducing loss.

Figure 2.5: equity curves based on reducing losses of 10 per cent and 2 per cent

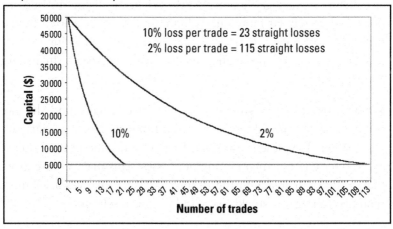

27

The 2 per cent risk rule

No first prizes for guessing which percentage successful share traders use. A 2 per cent reducing loss enables us to sustain more than 100 consecutive losses. Here's a tip: if you ever get to 100 consecutive losses then immediately stop trading and withdraw from the stock market: the strategy you're employing obviously isn't working. Share traders call this risk control method the 2 per cent risk rule. It states:

> Never risk more than 2 per cent of total capital on any individual trade.

I use the 2 per cent risk rule to manage my own superannuation portfolio, as well as my children's training portfolio (which is worth a lot less). And don't fall for the trap of thinking that a 1 per cent risk rule would be better than the 2 per cent risk rule. Using 1 per cent leads to other problems, such as over-diversification, which will hamper performance and increase management costs such as brokerage fees. You'll find that 2 per cent provides the optimal balance between risk control and diversification within a growth portfolio.

Assess or control

Unfortunately we can't apply the 2 per cent risk rule to our income portfolio or the property market, because they both operate on a different dynamic. Applying the 2 per cent risk rule requires the use of stop losses and, as you'll see in chapter 10, we don't employ stop losses to manage income shares. When managing our income portfolio, we rely far more on qualitative analysis, as Warren Buffett does. It's more a case of assessment, rather than controlling risk, by evaluating a company's management, future prospects, financials, and the like.

When a property investment goes awry, we usually find that we suffer a loss of time rather than a loss of money. This is because we are very much inclined towards riding out a decline in the value of our property rather than cutting our losses. This makes sense given that cutting our losses in the property market involves a lot more than just calling our stockbroker and placing a sell order.

So risk management in the property market leans towards risk assessment rather than risk control. Hence, a property investor mostly manages their risk by assessing all the relevant factors (such as the direction of interest rates and rental demand) before entering the market, whereas a share trader manages risk primarily by regulating their losses after they're in the market.

Systematic approach

For share traders (or growth investors), applying the 2 per cent risk rule is a must for long-term success. Furthermore, we can make the process of applying the 2 per cent risk rule entirely mechanical, which not only makes life easier but also allows us to keep our emotions and psychology out of the management process. A share trader doesn't study their portfolio and think, 'Gee, I wonder if I should sell that share?' They check to see if any of their stop losses have been breached and, if they have, they automatically sell.

In fact, share traders can automate their entire approach to managing their growth portfolio, including what to buy, when to buy it, how many shares to buy and when to sell. That's exactly what part II of this book is all about: I'm going to show you a complete blue chip share trading strategy, demonstrate how it works using historical market data, and then provide you with performance figures for the Australian stock market covering a 10-year period. And yes, the strategy did outperform the market—significantly.

PART II

Managing a blue chip share growth portfolio

Chapter 3

Introduction to growth shares

Imagine you were contemplating setting up your own chain of fast food restaurants, the idea being that you would ultimately franchise the business right across Australia and possibly overseas. But you're a sensible businessperson and you know that you need to start small and work your way up. After all, if you can't get one fast food restaurant up and running profitably then how would you ever hope to have a chain of them operating across the country?

You know step one is to perform a feasibility study of your proposed business concept and so you look around for a similar business model that is already being successfully implemented. There are several well-established businesses that fit the bill and so you move on to step two: conducting a thorough investigation of an existing fast food chain, so as to risk as little energy and money as possible. You work out all the information you need to gather and approach the business in question. Let's assume it's a local McDonald's franchise and you have the following questions at the ready:

- Can I please see your operations manuals and interview all your staff members?

- Can you give me copies of all your financial documents for the past five years, including your tax returns?

- Can I hang around in your restaurant for as long as I like to observe the day-to-day operations and count the number of customers who come and go each week?

- I'd also like to know what is the average dollar spend per customer?

- And speaking of customers, can I interview several dozen of them at random?

- Can you tell me what problems, if any, you've encountered when dealing with the franchisor since you started running the restaurant—and what did you actually pay for the franchise?

Of course, the only thing that the McDonald's franchisee is going to show you is the door. So even though undertaking a preliminary feasibility study is always a sensible idea, the ultimate acid test is to actually start your own restaurant and risk all the costs involved in doing so. Anyone in business will tell you that at the end of the day there really is no substitute for putting your own hard-earned money on the table and getting your feet wet.

Paper trading

But there is one business model that can be fully road-tested without you having to risk anything, and that's share trading. You can develop a trading system and implement it entirely on paper, for as long as you like, without having to risk a single cent. In fact, anyone who deals in growth stocks who hasn't taken full advantage of this unique feature of the stock market is taking unnecessary risks. Therefore, I recommend to anyone investing in growth stocks for the first time that they start by investing nothing.

Paper trade with pretend money—why not start with $1 million, for fun?—until you have achieved acceptable results and acquired enough confidence to put your real money at risk. To quantify what I mean by 'acceptable results', I aim to achieve a return on my investment capital of at least 20 per cent per year on average by committing no more than 20 minutes per week of my personal time. Figure 3.1 illustrates my blue chip share trading business model.

Figure 3.1: business model for Share Trading Pty Ltd

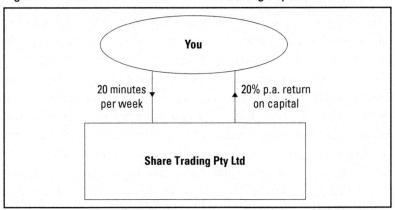

Blue chip

Let's now begin a closer examination of our shiny new share trading business by defining what we mean by the term *blue chip*. While this terminology is commonplace, there is in fact no specific definition of what a blue chip share is. Qualitatively speaking, some say it's a high-priced share, while others say it's a share that represents a large company, such as BHP, or a share that represents a quality company that has good future prospects and solid management. Most stock market participants would say it's a combination of all these factors.

Quantitatively speaking, the term *blue chip* has been used to define companies that are in the top 50 by market capitalisation:

market capitalisation = the current share price ×
the number of shares issued

The problem is that the term has also been used to identify the top 100, the top 200 and the top 500 companies. So, given all this confusion, for our purposes we will define blue chip shares as those that represent quality companies with large market capitalisation or, putting it more succinctly, all the companies included in the Standard & Poor's ASX 200 (S&P/ASX 200) index. By doing this we are piggybacking on the research of the Standard & Poor's organisation—a US company that analyses stocks and bonds—and saving ourselves a lot of work.

Process not product

The shares we buy and sell are our product, so to speak, and our focus in the stock market should be as it is in business: the focus is on the process rather than the product. Hence when investing in growth stocks we should focus on our trading system and not the shares we buy and sell. Mind you, it's a very different story when it comes to income stocks, but with growth stocks, they are just our stock in trade. To reinforce the importance of not taking a product-based approach to the market when dealing in growth stocks, let's take a look at one of the most commonly used product-based approaches that usually doesn't work, namely, 'buy low, sell high'. Exponents of this approach can often be heard saying (or should that be lamenting?), 'the share price should go up'.

Hunting for a bargain is a good way to approach buying a toaster or a new television but it is a very impractical way to approach share trading. I had a phone call from one of my brokers (I use several) back when the Lend Lease share price fell from just over $22 to $17 way back in early 2001, suggesting that the then price of the shares was very cheap. His precise words were, 'Lend Lease shares are at a bargain price and now is a great time to buy them—they can only go one way from here, and that's up'. Figure 3.2 illustrates how Lend Lease got to $17 a share.

Figure 3.2: Lend Lease at $17

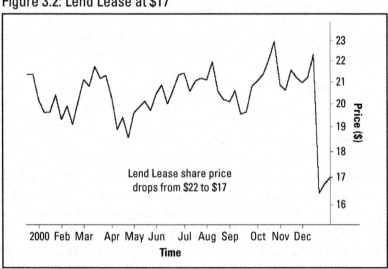

Source: MetaStock.

About two months later, the price of Lend Lease shares fell even further—down by another $2 to $15. What's more, the broker had the audacity to ring me again, saying this was definitely the bargain of a lifetime (see figure 3.3).

Figure 3.3: Lend Lease at $15

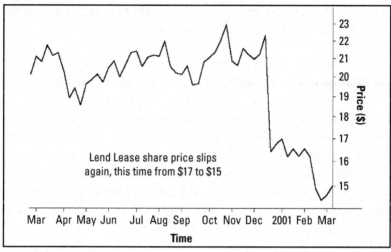

Source: MetaStock.

But Lend Lease shares continued to fall, until they dipped below $11, as shown in figure 3.4.

Figure 3.4: Lend Lease at $11

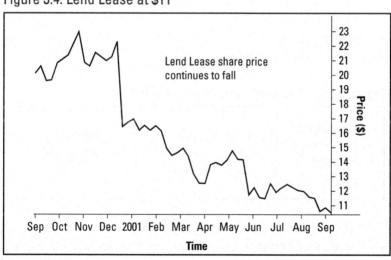

Source: MetaStock.

There's no such thing as a bargain-priced share: a share's price is always the precise value that all market participants collectively place on it at that exact moment. What the broker is really saying is that the sentiment surrounding Lend Lease is abnormally low and should improve from this point. The problem with this approach is that there is no telling when sentiment is likely to improve and if, in fact, it is likely to improve at all. The broker is trying to pick the market bottom for Lend Lease and has failed miserably—largely at the expense of his clients.

I can only spot highs and lows in the stock market with the benefit of hindsight, and attempting to apply the theory of 'buy low, sell high' in real time would mean being able to see into the future. This is bargain hunting through individual share analysis and it is a very hit-and-miss approach to share trading. What's more, it isn't what Warren Buffett does, because he's buying a rising income yield and not a falling share price—but that's a story for later on. However, as share traders we are buying and selling share price, and the correct approach is to 'buy a rising share, sell a falling share'—which is almost the exact opposite of 'buy low, sell high'.

An active approach

Now let's look at how the stock market really works. In the simplest possible way, figure 3.5 shows how and why share prices move up and down. Factors that affect opinion are released into the public domain and you and I, as individual investors or collectively through managed funds, react to this information by either buying up or selling down the share price.

Figure 3.5: how and why prices rise and fall

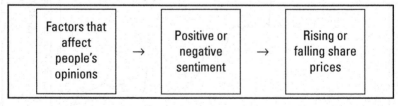

| Factors that affect people's opinions | → | Positive or negative sentiment | → | Rising or falling share prices |

Factors that affect opinion include a company's asset backing, its debt level, its earnings growth, its profitability, its future prospects, its management and a lot more. These factors can be summed up by describing them as a company's fundamentals. Many other factors also affect opinion, such as the behaviour of the US stock market, local and overseas interest rates, and the price of crude oil. But undoubtedly the number one factor that most affects people's collective opinion about an individual company, and therefore has the greatest influence over its share price, is its fundamentals. The block diagram in figure 3.6 describes a philosophy that is very widely accepted and used when it comes to investing in growth shares.

Figure 3.6: why prices rise over time

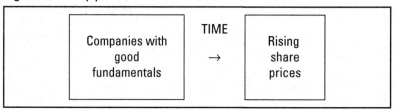

If we buy companies with good fundamentals, given the passage of time the share price will inevitably rise. This is another product-based approach which is commonly referred to as *value investing*. This trading technique does work but, once again, it is a bit hit and miss and leaves the door open to a lot of subjective analysis. What's more, it is actually possible to eliminate the time factor and achieve the same result, as shown in figure 3.7.

Figure 3.7: the effect of eliminating time

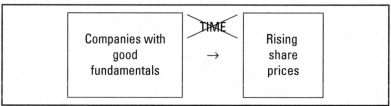

Value investing is largely a passive approach to share trading where you buy shares in an undervalued company and sit on them until the share price rises; it could take weeks (very unlikely), months (possible) or even years (very likely). So why not take an active approach and buy shares in fundamentally sound companies where the share price is already rising, thus eliminating the need to wait? You don't have to look for shares that are going down in price or even sideways in price to find ones that represent fundamentally sound companies. Figures 3.8 (Origin Energy) and 3.9 (Boral) are price charts for fundamentally sound companies where the share price had been rising for years. These are both well-known blue chip shares.

Figure 3.8: Origin Energy Ltd

Source: MetaStock.

Figure 3.9: Boral Ltd

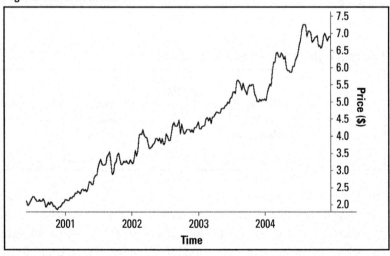

Source: MetaStock.

By testing and measuring price activity, we can eliminate the need to wait for share prices to go up. What's more, we don't have to do any company research if we don't want to, because if we stick to only those companies that are included in the S&P/ASX 200 index then it is reasonable to assume that they are fundamentally sound and institutionally backed.

But if it is so simple then why isn't everybody doing it? Because, as stated earlier, the conventional approach that has been accepted for many decades is to trade solely on a company's fundamentals and largely ignore its share price movement. The conventional approach does work and will continue to do so but, as some boutique fund managers are now proving, the results from trading a company's fundamentals and testing and measuring its share price activity are a lot more profitable. While the two approaches are unquestionably interrelated, at the end of the day, as share traders we profit from buying and selling the share price and not a company's fundamentals.

Being above average

Another commonly held yet spurious line of thinking is that it's impossible to beat the market averages over time. Luckily for me, my father, who was also a share trader, taught me that if you can't beat the market average, that is, the index, then don't bother trying: you may as well put your money with an index funds manager, as they can achieve the market average for you. So my mindset has always been that I can beat the market average, and it's particularly easy if we are using a trend-following approach to trading shares. Consider the following series of three numbers:

2 4 6—the average is 4.

In order to beat the average of four, we would have to manipulate this simple series of three numbers by eliminating the lowest value, namely two. We would therefore have:

__ 4 6—the average is now 5.

This method of beating the average is incredibly simple, and fortunately we can apply the same logic to beating a market index such as the S&P/ASX 200. But before we tackle the S&P/ASX 200, let's pretend we've created our own index that includes only four individual stocks. Two of our four member stocks are trending up, while the other two are trending down, as can be seen in figure 3.10.

Figure 3.10: four trending stocks and an index

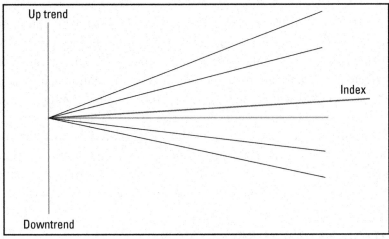

The index in figure 3.10 is an average of all four trends and is trending slightly upwards. Now, applying the same method we used in the numeric example earlier, you can see in figure 3.11 the impact on our index of eliminating both the downtrending stocks.

Figure 3.11: two trending stocks and an index

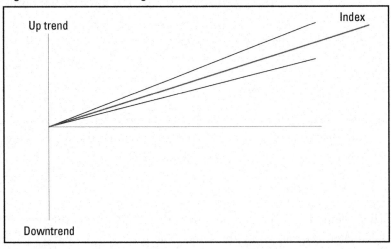

Now let's look at a real-world example of eliminating a downtrending stock from the S&P/ASX 200 index, which is made up of 200

constituent stocks of different weightings, depending on their market capitalisation. One of these 200 stocks is Telstra, and figure 3.12 shows how its share price fell 18.7 per cent during calendar year 2010.

Figure 3.12: Telstra's share price fell 18.7 per cent in 2010

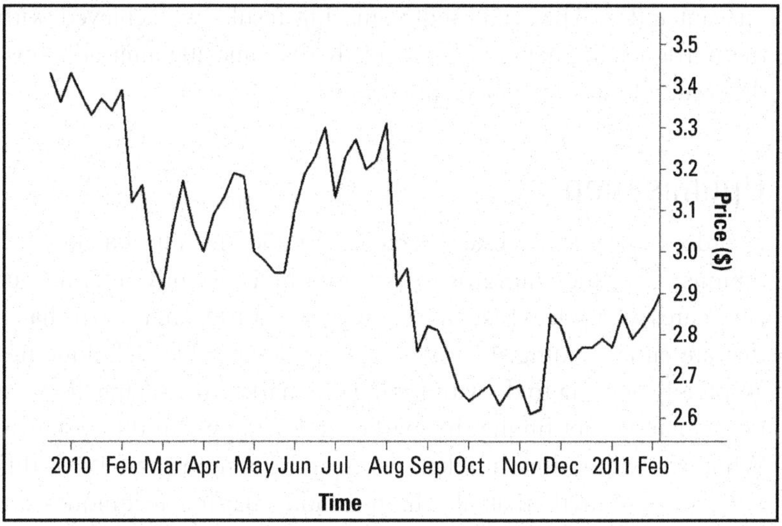

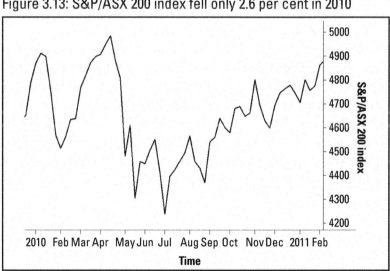

Source: MetaStock.

Figure 3.13 shows the S&P/ASX 200 index fell by just 2.6 per cent during the same period.

Figure 3.13: S&P/ASX 200 index fell only 2.6 per cent in 2010

Source: MetaStock.

Logic dictates that if we had purchased every stock that made up the S&P/ASX 200 index minus Telstra, then we would have beaten the average — albeit by an insignificantly small margin. As a trend trader, I simply take this logic to its extreme and purchase a portfolio of no more than 10 stocks that are all trending up much faster than the relevant index. The supposedly amazing results we achieved with the portfolios in chapter 1 aren't really that amazing after all — just the result of mathematical common sense.

Optimisation

In order to beat the market averages, I employ technical analysis to optimise my blue chip growth portfolio by constantly filtering out any shares with prices that aren't going up. I don't want to own shares that are either trading sideways or going down. This technique has absolutely nothing to do with timing the market: the saying 'It's time in the market, not timing the market' doesn't apply in this instance. While we will address market cycles and timing in part IV of this book, it is a myth that all chartists and charting techniques are attempting to time the market.

Active funds management

Maintaining a portfolio of fundamentally sound blue chip stocks where the share price is rising at an acceptable rate of return is a type of active funds management. This chapter has looked at the key concepts behind active funds management; the next two chapters describe, in detail, a specific trading technique that the average DIY investor who has had little to no prior exposure to fundamental or technical analysis can employ. This trading technique is a simple and robust trend-following approach that uses all the constituent stocks in the S&P/ASX 200 index as its universe. Typical examples of the sort of stocks we want to identify and own can be seen in figures 3.14 to 3.18 on the following pages.

Figure 3.14: Iluka Resources Ltd, 2010–11

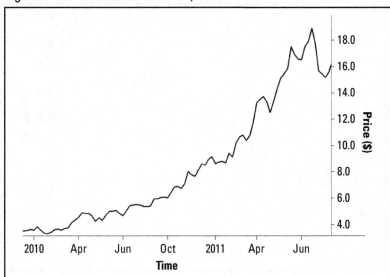

Source: MetaStock.

Figure 3.15: CSL Ltd, 2003–08

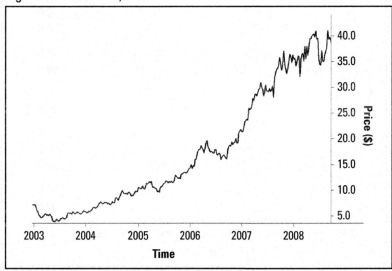

Source: MetaStock.

Figure 3.16: Cochlear Ltd, 2009–11

Source: MetaStock.

Figure 3.17: Blackmores Ltd, 2009–11

Source: MetaStock.

Figure 3.18: Ramsay Healthcare Ltd, 2009–12

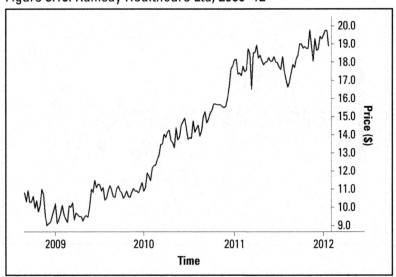

Source: MetaStock.

Active funds management embraces the single most important concept that I can teach anyone when it comes to managing a growth portfolio: if a share price is trending upwards, then the balance of probability suggests it will continue to do so. The problem is that this concept is too simple and very few of us complicated human beings are capable of adhering to simple truths. What's more, there's another problem to contend with—the losses.

It's easy but it's hard!

This is the hard part. The science of share trading is simple, but the psychological aspect can be very hard. Figures 3.14 to 3.18 paint a very rosy picture of increasing prices, but there will be losses to contend with as well. Although the 2 per cent risk rule acts as our safety net, we still need to have the stomach for probability. While tipping the scale of probability in our favour will inevitably lead to success (read: profits), it doesn't mean that we'll enjoy win after win after win.

To illustrate my point let's go back to the simple game of tossing a coin. As before, we can see the results of 100 consecutive coin tosses as shown in figure 3.19 (overleaf), showing 'balance of outcomes'.

Figure 3.19: results for 100 coin tosses

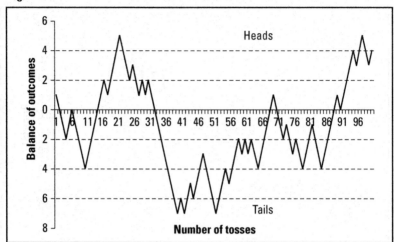

Now, while the probable outcome of tossing a coin is an even split between heads and tails, it doesn't mean that the outcome will oscillate perfectly between heads and tails in a flip-flop head–tail–head–tail pattern. However, it does mean that the balance of outcomes will always return to the baseline of zero. But as we know from figure 3.19, the outcome can deviate by as much as seven, and it's this deviation that can be hard to stomach.

Let's assume that you are betting on tails in our game of coin toss, and so you are down by five tosses after the 21st game. In other words, you have lost 13 games and won only eight. At this point, most people will want to inspect the coin and maybe have a turn at tossing it for a while.

Now miraculously the odds swing in your favour and you find that you're ahead by seven tosses at the end of the 39th game. Of course, your opponent is now the one beginning to question the fairness of the game and whether or not the probable outcome is in fact 50–50.

But just to make matters worse, let's assume that you don't actually get to witness the game of coin toss. Both players are simply being given the results of the game, played at a remote location, by a supposedly reliable third party, such as the Australian Securities Exchange. Now ask yourself: if you were down 13 losses to eight wins in a game where you were playing for $5000 per toss, would you drop out of the game because you believed it was unfairly biased?

Testing times

Unfortunately this is an all too common occurrence in the stock market, particularly during tough times, when a string of eight consecutive losses, or even more, is quite possible. I've seen some individuals who prove a share trading strategy through comprehensive back testing, only to dismiss it as a failure after trading it in real time for as few as 10 trades. It seems they just don't have the stomach for probability. Their ability to maintain their mathematical objectivity is lost because their hip-pocket nerves eventually override all other thinking by transmitting ever-increasing pain signals to the brain.

As mentioned earlier we can fully test any market strategy by either back testing or executing it in real time without risking a cent by paper trading for a statistically significant period of time. A statistically significant period of time means a period that includes at least 30 discrete bits of data, as this is the smallest sample that can be considered in any way valid; the mathematical proof of this can be found in any good textbook on statistical analysis. If we're analysing share prices on a weekly basis then our minimum testing period would be 30 weeks, and so on. And rest assured that you will probably witness many losses during these testing times.

It is a well-accepted fact among successful share traders that a streak of eight consecutive losses is not uncommon. This is why the ability to sustain losses is so important, not only in terms of your trading capital but also with respect to your psychological capital. To preserve your trading capital, I recommend sticking to the 2 per cent risk rule. To preserve your psychological capital I recommend carrying a coin at all times—you never know when you might have to play a game of coin toss and prove to yourself that a string of eight consecutive losses is very possible.

Chapter 4

Rules for entering the market

The trading system described in the next two chapters employs all of the principles covered in the previous chapter. While this system is by no means the only solution to managing a blue chip growth portfolio, it is a working system that demonstrates how key concepts are put to practical use. It is broken down into two distinct parts: this chapter looks at which shares to buy, while chapter 5 describes the more critical matter of when to sell—an aspect of share trading that is often dangerously underrated by many market participants.

Almost everyone I meet seems to have some idea of what shares to buy, and they're usually only too willing to pass this information on to anyone who will listen. But, unfortunately, very few people will let you know when it's a good time to sell. Have you ever had a friend who gave you a stock market tip ring back later on to say, 'Sorry mate, things haven't gone the way I expected and I reckon you should get out now'? Not a very common occurrence. Hence, the following bit of advice is one of the best tips anyone ever gave me: Free advice is usually worth what you pay for it.

The reality is it's much easier to know when to buy than it is to know when to sell. Furthermore, success with growth shares mainly comes from good management of the shares you own, rather than good share selection. A group of traders in the US, called the Turtle Traders, proved that they could trade profitably by using strict risk management and random stock selection. Don't misunderstand me: we'll be using good share selection and good risk management as we're trying to generate lots of profits and money, not prove a point. So let's get down to business and, as investing in growth shares is primarily about capitalising on price movement, we need to return to the science of technical analysis.

Moving averages

At the end of chapter 1, I introduced you to price charts, and now we need to delve a bit deeper into the chartist's toolbox, starting with the most basic indicator: the simple moving average (SMA). Because week-to-week price movements can bounce around quite considerably, it is very helpful to use a moving average to smooth out the price activity, removing the unwanted effect of short-term volatility. The moving average for any given week can be easily calculated by adding together the closing prices of 'X' number of weeks, up to and including the given week, and then dividing this sum by 'X'.

The following formula can be used to calculate the average price for a five-week period where week one would be the most recent week, and week two would be the week before that, and so on.

$$5 \text{ week average} = (\text{closing price for week } 1 + \text{week } 2 + \text{week } 3 + \text{week } 4 + \text{week } 5) \div 5$$

In using this method we are calculating what is referred to as the simple average for any given five-week period. As each new week occurs the simple average can be recalculated and then all the averages, which are plotted as a series of points on a price chart, can be connected using a single unbroken line that is referred to, appropriately, as a *simple moving average*.

A 30-week simple moving average (grey line) is shown in the price chart for Company A in figure 4.1.

Figure 4.1: Company A — 30-week simple moving average

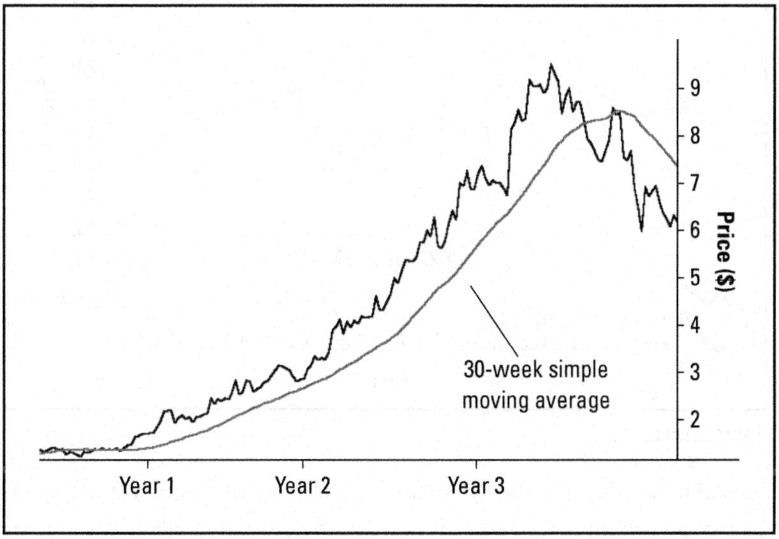

Source: MetaStock.

Curve fitting

The SMA has been in use by chartists since the early 1900s and it is readily available today through many internet-based broking services and charting programs. With this one basic charting tool at our disposal we are now ready to start analysing shares. The first task we have to perform is to curve-fit an SMA to each share we wish to study by adjusting the time period; for example, by changing it from 15 weeks to 16 weeks and so on.

We want the moving average to reflect the behaviour of the underlying price activity. This is done by varying the time period that will directly affect the position of the SMA line. We want to make the line sit just under, while not quite touching, the price activity for a time span slightly greater than 12 months. The SMA line in figure 4.2 (overleaf) sits just under the price activity for a duration of more than 12 months when the time period is set to 22 weeks.

Figure 4.2: Company A — curve-fitted moving average

These lines are 12 months apart

A 22-week SMA fits just nicely

Jan Feb Mar Apr May Jun Jul Aug Sep Oct Nov Dec Jan

Time

Price ($)

3.6
3.4
3.2
3.0
2.8
2.6
2.4
2.2
2.0
1.8
1.6
1.4

Source: MetaStock.

You can see that the moving average line, while reducing the effect of price volatility very effectively, does accurately reflect the overall trend in Company A over the 12-month period indicated on the chart in figure 4.2. Note that the time frame of 12 months is no accident: this is the actual time frame that we want to operate in, so it is the minimum period of time that we need to analyse. What's more, we can use any period up to 52 weeks for the moving average, because this maximum parameter (upper tolerance limit) is also determined by our chosen time frame.

As we are exclusively interested in shares where the price activity is trending upwards, we can conveniently eliminate any shares where a 52-week SMA, which generates the most tolerant line, won't fit under at least 12 months of price activity. This can be seen in figure 4.3, which shows the price chart of Company B with an SMA using our maximum time period of 52 weeks, where the price activity is trending more sideways than up. We would immediately dismiss Company B as a potential trading opportunity given that it's not an upward-trending share.

Figure 4.3: Company B — sideways price activity

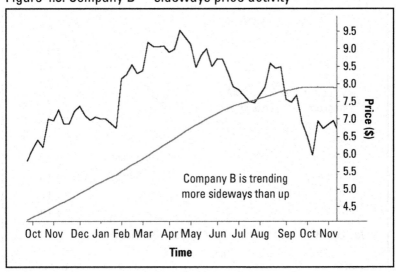

Source: MetaStock.

Rate of annual return

Once we've separated out only those stocks that are included in the S&P/ASX 200 index and are trending upwards, we then need to compare them with each other. To do this we must measure their rates of annual return, which we will refer to as their ROAR. A share's ROAR, which is a proportional measurement, is calculated using the current value of a curve-fitted SMA and its current trend, where the trend is defined as the rate of change in value in the SMA over the past year.

It sounds a bit daunting but by studying figure 4.4 (overleaf) and its corresponding calculation, you'll see that it's a reasonably straightforward process. Using the Company A chart from figure 4.2, we need to note the current value of the 22-week SMA and the value of the 22-week SMA from one year ago.

Figure 4.4: Company A—rate of return

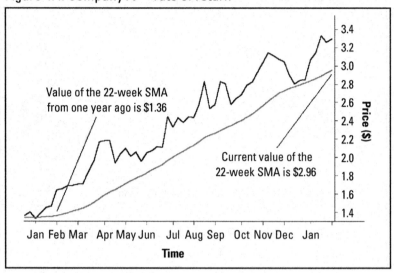

Source: MetaStock.

ROAR calculation

Using just these two figures from the 22-week SMA we can determine the following:

- the rate of change in price over the past year = $2.96 – $1.36 = $1.60

- the rate of annual return as a percentage = 100 × ($1.60 ÷ $2.96) = 54%

This calculation gives the share's current rate of return, which is the growth we would anticipate if we purchased it now. And it is also an approximation based on the moving average rather than directly on the share price itself. Hence if we bought shares in Company A today at $3.30 (the current share price, shown in figure 4.4) and the trend continued to be a rise of $1.60 per year, then we would enjoy an annual return of 100 × ($1.60 ÷ $3.30) = 48%. That's slightly less than 54 per cent, but still a fairly good approximation.

Told you it was fairly straightforward. Now all we have to do is perform the same process for all the rising shares included in the S&P/ASX 200 index. I didn't say it wasn't boring, but there are alternatives to doing these measurements and calculations manually, as you will see in chapter 6 when I introduce you to my weekly *Blue Chip Report*. But assuming we were to do this process manually, it would have to be repeated at regular intervals of no greater than one month in order for the ROAR readings to remain up to date and valid.

Let's now assume that we've finished analysing all the rising shares in the S&P/ASX 200 and tabulated their ROARs. We can now prioritise them according to their anticipated profitability. The next step is a little more involved, as we need to consider several factors at once when deciding what is the minimum amount of profit we are prepared to accept from the stock market — an important consideration if we don't want our bank balances to go backwards.

Minimum rate of annual return (the cut-off ROAR)

In order to determine the lowest tolerable rate of annual return (or cut-off ROAR), we first need to ascertain what ROAR represents the break-even point, because in fact it is not a ROAR of zero. Before that, we need to estimate the average life expectancy of a typical trade — how long we are likely to hold each share. Interestingly, this parameter is also largely a consequence of our chosen time frame of 12 months because share prices love to trend up and down for fairly predictable periods of time. The real-world example of Burns, Philp and Company in figure 4.5 (overleaf) shows a share price trending up and down at regular intervals.

Figure 4.5: Burns, Philp and Company — cyclical behaviour

Source: MetaStock.

Another predictable feature is that the periodicity of these trends is usually three months, six months, one year, two years and so on. Based on this anticipated trend behaviour, we can reasonably deduce that if a share has trended up for just over one year then it will probably continue to trend until it reaches two years in duration, a period of slightly less than 12 months. Now, if you refer back to the earlier section in this chapter on curve fitting (see p. 53), you will note that I said the SMA should sit just under, while not quite touching, the price activity for a time *slightly greater* than 12 months.

This brings us to the estimate of the average life expectancy of a trend being *slightly less* than 12 months, which, for practical purposes, we will approximate to be one year.

As you will shortly see, using an estimate in this instance is acceptable, given that we are using it to determine a very helpful but non-critical aspect of our strategy — the break-even ROAR.

The next parameter we need to take into account is our stop loss (the price at which we must sell the share), which is very simply a 20 per cent drawdown from the highest closing price in the past 12 months. The 20 per cent drawdown price level can be represented by a line on a price chart, as seen in the following chart of Company A in figure 4.6. You can see how the 20 per cent drawdown level, which is our stop loss, moves up each time the price activity makes a new high. Notice, however, that the stop loss doesn't fall when price activity retreats, thus locking in profits as the trend progresses. But if we factor in a life expectancy of 12 months per trade, and knowing that our exit criterion (the point where we will sell the share) is a 20 per cent drawdown stop loss, then a rate of annual return of zero will in fact result in a 20 per cent loss over one year.

Figure 4.6: Company A — 20 per cent drawdown stop loss

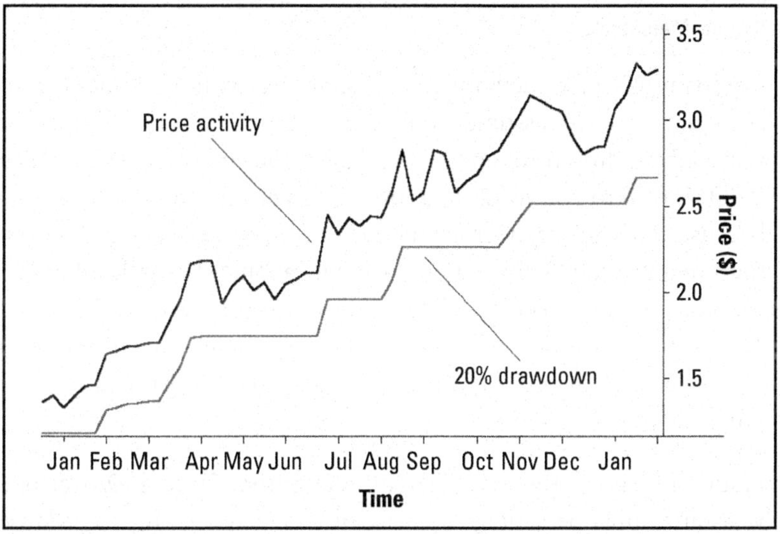

Source: MetaStock.

The hypothetical chart for Company C in figure 4.7 (overleaf), where price moves horizontally with a ROAR of zero, illustrates the inevitable outcome of a 20 per cent loss.

Figure 4.7: Company C—0 per cent rate of annual return

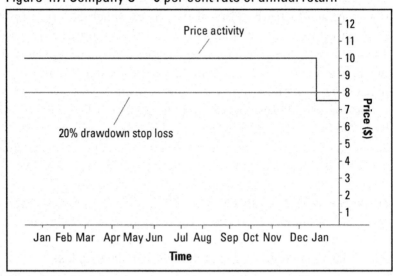

Source: MetaStock.

Company C's price activity moves sideways with a ROAR of zero at the level we can assume we bought it at of $10 at the start of the year, only to drop through the stop loss at the end of the year. Hence a ROAR of zero will result in a loss of 20 per cent in one year's time because our exit signal from the trade is a 20 per cent drawdown that we anticipate will occur, on average, about 12 months after our time of purchase. Therefore, to achieve a break-even result over a 12-month period, the minimum percentage increase would have to be 25 per cent in order to offset the inevitable 20 per cent drop to our stop loss.

Figure 4.8 shows the price activity rising from $8 to $10 over one year (an annual percentage increase of 25 per cent), only to collapse back through $8 at the end of the year.

Our 20 per cent drawdown stop loss tracks along 20 per cent behind the price activity, climbing to $8 when the price activity rises to $10, approximately one year after it started trending up—a break-even result. Now that we have determined our break-even ROAR, we must add to it a rate of return that we would accept as a bare minimum return from our blue chip growth portfolio as a whole.

Figure 4.8: price increase of 25 per cent per annum

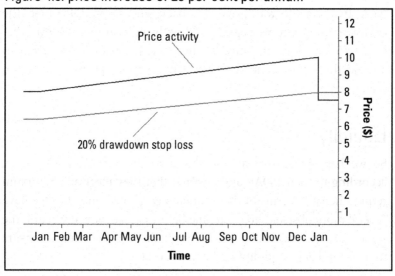

Source: MetaStock.

Personally, I won't expose myself to the general risk of owning equities unless I can achieve at least the same rate of return I would achieve from a cash investment. Therefore, my minimum return from the stock market would need to be at least the Reserve Bank of Australia's (RBA's) cash interest rate target, which can be found at <www.rba.gov.au>.

At the time of writing the RBA cash rate target is 3.75 per cent, and so the minimum rate of annual return that I can tolerate when buying my blue chip shares is the break-even ROAR of 25 per cent plus the RBA cash rate target of 3.75 per cent: 28.75 per cent.

There are two important points worth noting now. The first is that the RBA cash rate target will also be affected by our 20 per cent drawdown stop loss, but the resulting impact will be relatively insignificant and can therefore be ignored. As stated earlier, this is not a mission-critical benchmark, and we have already employed several approximations well before reaching this late stage of the calculation anyway.

The second point is that our strategy is to buy a share at, say, $10, and watch it reach a high of about $13 over the next 12-month period, only to sell when it falls all the way back down to about

$10.50. The reality of share trading is two steps forward, one step back; two steps forward, one step back; and so on. Of course, the numbers used here were generated with the minimum ROAR, that is, 28.75 per cent, and buying shares with rates of annual return around the 40 per cent to 50 per cent level is a far more common scenario.

Liquidity

So we have prioritised all the shares in the S&P/ASX 200 index according to their ROAR and ensured that they meet our minimum requirements in terms of their anticipated profitability. But we have several more obstacles to overcome before we can actually get on the phone to our stockbroker. The first of these is the need to ensure there is sufficient liquidity in the marketplace.

If you think of trading shares as being no different from trading any other commodity, then one of the great advantages of share trading is that there is always a ready supply of both buyers and sellers. But it is possible to exhaust this supply if we don't ensure an adequate number of shares are being traded in the marketplace before we enter it. This supply of shares is commonly referred to as liquidity and it is defined as the number of shares traded over any given period, or the value of shares traded over any given period. For example:

- If 1 million shares were bought and sold over one week then the liquidity would be 1 million shares per week.

- If these shares traded at an average price of $10 over the course of a given week then the liquidity in terms of value ($) would be 1 million × $10: $10 million per week.

The liquidity in terms of value is also referred to as cash flow, and it is this statistic that is of most interest to us. Without going into great detail, we need to ensure that our purchases or sales of any particular stock do not exceed 5 per cent of the average weekly cash flow. This somewhat conservative benchmark will guarantee that we will always enjoy an easy passage either into or out of the marketplace, as we intend to take up to two weeks to enter or exit any given trade. For example:

- Assuming an average of 400 000 shares in Company A were traded each week at an average value of $10 each, then the average weekly cash flow would be $4 million.

- Therefore, 5 per cent of the average weekly cash flow would be 0.05 × $4 million, which equals $200 000. Hence we would purchase no more than $200 000 worth of Company A's shares.

In the event that a stock has insufficient liquidity we should overlook it and move on, as there will always be others to choose from. By ensuring that our purchases represent no more than 5 per cent of the weekly turnover in any particular stock, we will never find ourselves in the embarrassing situation of not having enough buyers or sellers to trade with, which is a bit like working in an overstocked retail store that rarely has any customers.

Diversification

Another embarrassing situation that is common to both share trading and running a retail shop is not having a wide enough variety of stock, or insufficient diversification.

In a retail business this would mean having to turn away many potential customers because we can't sell them what they want. In the stock market it is a little more serious, as a lack of diversification exposes us to unnecessary risk. If we own too many shares in stocks that belong to a particular industrial sector then we become vulnerable to what is technically referred to as sector-specific risk. It sounds fancy but all it really means is that we have too many eggs in the one industrial basket.

Anyone who has studied the Australian stock market over a period of several years will have observed the propensity of individual industrial sectors to run hot or cold at different times. Some examples of this would be the resources and energy sectors in the 2000s and the technology sector during the late 1990s. But in the stock market, as in life, all good things must come to an end and, although we've seen some industrial sectors run hot for periods of up to several years, they inevitably cool off.

It is this cooling-off phase that has a tendency to hurt our bank accounts, and so we have to seek a balance between being able to capitalise on a hot sector and not overexposing ourselves to the sector-specific risk that comes with it. Given that a stock market correction is defined as being a 10 per cent to 20 per cent fall in value, and a crash is defined as being at least a 20 per cent fall in value, we would be reducing the impact of a sector crash to less than that of a correction if it were to affect well under half of our portfolio's total value.

In other words, it would be very sensible to own a maximum of only four stocks from any one particular industrial group. Hence if all four stocks that belonged to a single sector were to stop out (hit their stop loss price) then we would suffer a loss of four times our individual position risk of 2 per cent, which would be a total loss of 8 per cent. Not a desirable outcome, but hardly a catastrophic one either. The Australian Securities Exchange (ASX) provides the industry group for all publicly listed companies at its website <www.asx.com.au>. Simply look up the company's share code in the 'Company research' section.

The top 10

Our efforts to this point, given average market conditions, will have yielded a list of approximately 50 to 60 potential trading opportunities from which we can now select our portfolio of just the top 10 stocks by their rate of annual return. Of course, don't forget to ensure that the top 10 stocks don't include more than four companies from the same industrial sector. In the event this does occur, which is quite likely, simply eliminate any unwanted stocks from the overall list by culling those that have the lowest rate of annual return.

There is a very good reason for our portfolio to contain exactly 10 individual positions—this is a direct consequence of the combination of our stop loss and our maximum tolerance of risk. Here's the clever bit: if the stop loss is a 20 per cent drop in the price of any share, and we want to remain faithful to the 2 per cent risk rule as described in chapter 2, then we must allocate no more than 10 per cent of our total capital to any individual position. The reason for this is very simple: 20 per cent of 10 per cent equals 2 per cent.

Let's assume our total capital is $1 million and we're going to have 10 equal positions. Here's how our portfolio would work:

- We'll buy $100 000 worth of shares in Company A because $100 000 is 10 per cent of $1 million.
- If we sell our shares in Company A when they drop by 20 per cent then we will have lost $20 000.
- As $20 000 represents 2 per cent of $1 million, we will have lost only 2 per cent of our total capital.

Also note that suffering a 20 per cent drawdown from our actual purchase price is a worst case scenario, because we will only occasionally buy shares when they're making new highs. So now you can see that there is a very good reason for buying 10 equally proportioned positions when using a drawdown stop loss of 20 per cent — it's the appropriate balance between performance and protection according to the 2 per cent risk rule.

Checklist of steps

All the steps that we take in deciding what stocks to buy, and how many to buy, can be seen as a series of filters. Some of them are designed to optimise our portfolio's profitability, while others are there to safeguard our financial wellbeing. By breaking the management process down into a sequence of virtually mechanical steps like this, we go a long way towards eliminating the need for discretion.

This is a good thing because the less discretion we use, the less emotion can creep into the process. Running any sort of business should be an objective exercise and not one directed by personal whims. And just like any other well-run business, it's always a sensible idea to have an operations-manual-cum-checklist to manage the day-to-day operations — or, in this case, the week-to-week operations.

Here are the steps or filters we followed.

✓ *Curve-fit an SMA.* Adjust the period of a simple moving average so it sits just under the line showing slightly more than 12 months of price activity.

✓ *Measure the ROAR.* Using the SMA, calculate the rate of annual return for every stock in the S&P/ASX 200 index and prioritise them accordingly.

✓ *Set cut-off ROAR.* Determine the minimum acceptable rate of annual return using the sum of the break-even ROAR (25 per cent) and the current RBA cash rate target.

✓ *Measure liquidity.* Calculate 5 per cent of the average weekly turnover of each individual share in terms of its cash flow (volume × average price).

✓ *Buy the top 10.* Take the top 10 stocks from the list, ensuring that there are no more than four stocks from any particular industry, and that and the liquidity in terms of cash flow is acceptable in each case.

Hey presto: we've now created a blue chip growth portfolio using five relatively simple steps.

Up to this point, most people consider share trading to be a lot of fun—a hunting exercise of sorts. But now it's time to move on to the serious bit: what to do once we've bought our shares.

Chapter 5

Rules for exiting the market

If buying shares was considered to be climbing a mountain, then we are about to start our way back down the other side by establishing a set of reasons and criteria for selling our growth shares. If this all seems a bit much to take in at first glance then rest assured, you're not alone. I certainly wouldn't be able to digest an entire trading strategy in the time it takes to read several chapters of a book, and that's why I've dedicated the next chapter to putting it all into practice.

There is much learning in the doing, and often the science begins to make much more sense to us when we start to convert it into action.

Our checklist, which we started in the previous chapter, is our link between the theory and the practice of managing a blue chip growth portfolio—a link that is about to expand rapidly as we delve into the many reasons for selling our shares.

20 per cent drawdown stop loss

Buying shares is relatively quick and easy compared with managing the shares that we already own. One of the reasons for this imbalance is that there are actually more criteria for selling shares than there are for buying, and the obvious one for us to start with is the 20 per cent drawdown stop loss that we've already discussed at some length in the previous chapter. The price chart for Company A shown in figure 5.1 shows how the 20 per cent drawdown stop loss tracks along 20 per cent below Company A's highest closing price.

Figure 5.1: Company A — 20 per cent drawdown stop loss

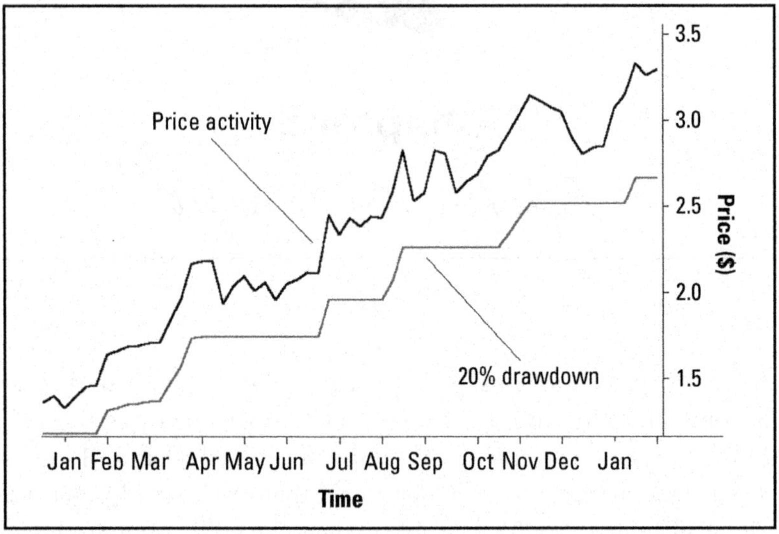

Source: MetaStock.

So the first addition to our checklist on the selling side is:

> *20 per cent drawdown stop loss: sell if the price activity draws down more than 20 per cent from the highest price in the last 12 months.*

Moving average stop loss

This stop loss is actually the flip side of one of our entry conditions. Remember that we determined that the maximum period for our curve-fitted SMA was 52 weeks. Therefore we can infer that if a share's price activity were to close below the 52-week SMA then we should sell it. In figure 5.2 I have simply added a 52-week SMA to the Company A chart shown in figure 5.1. If a share price is trending upwards at a reasonable speed, then the 52-week SMA will typically be well below the 20 per cent drawdown stop loss. But if the share price is moving up slowly then the SMA stop loss will actually be higher than the drawdown stop loss, as can be seen near the left-hand edge of figure 5.2 for Company A. It is therefore necessary to employ both stop losses—the 20 per cent drawdown stop loss and the moving average stop loss—simultaneously. Therefore the next addition to our checklist is:

> *Moving average stop loss: sell if the share price drops below the 52-week SMA.*

Figure 5.2: Company A—moving average and 20 per cent drawdown stop losses

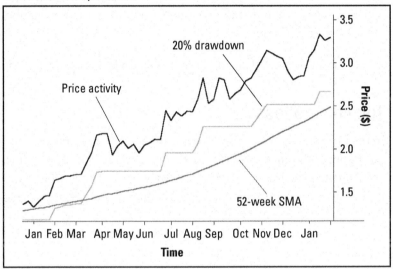

Source: MetaStock.

ROAR stop loss (exit rate of annual return)

We now need to determine at what point the rate of annual return becomes unacceptable to us, and this is different to our minimum entry rate of annual return. In fact, our exit rate of annual return is the break-even ROAR, which we have already determined in the previous chapter to be 25 per cent. While we want to buy shares that will yield at least the RBA cash rate target, we are prepared to hold onto shares until they drop below the break-even threshold. What's more, these two values cannot be identical, because that will create a very irritating side effect.

Imagine for a moment that our minimum entry ROAR and our stop loss ROAR were both set at 30 per cent. Then if a share's ROAR were to rise up to 30 per cent we would buy it, but immediately sell if it dropped down to 29 per cent, as that would constitute a breach of our ROAR stop loss. Then if it rose back to 30 per cent we would buy it again and then if it dropped to 29 per cent we would sell it again, and so on. Using the same minimum entry ROAR and stop loss ROAR will introduce an unwanted instability into our strategy—we need to set these two parameters significantly apart from each other.

So by setting the ROAR stop loss to the break-even ROAR, the RBA cash rate target acts as a buffer between our entry and exit ROARs, which will provide our trading system with the necessary stability. Our next exit rule reads:

ROAR stop loss: sell if the rate of annual return falls below 25 per cent.

Top 40 stop loss

In the previous chapter, we placed our money on the 10 fastest rising stocks out of the entire S&P/ASX 200 index, using their ROAR values as a yardstick. But as time has a tendency to erode a stock's rate of return (all trends must come to an end sooner or later), time will also inevitably eat away at a stock's top-10 ranking. So in the same vein as our ROAR stop loss, we need to determine a minimum ranking benchmark that is set a considerable distance away from our entry criteria for the top 10 stocks.

This is really an exercise in optimisation rather than risk management, so we have the luxury of setting the minimum ranking at any level we like, providing it doesn't lead to any unwanted instability. Given that our total population is 200 stocks, a conservative balance would be to set the minimum ranking at 40 (the top 20 per cent of the S&P/ASX 200 index), which is a comfortable distance away from our entry criteria of the top 10.

The next reason for selling shares is:

Top 40 stop loss: sell if a stock's rate of annual return falls outside the rate of annual return of the top 40 stocks.

At this point you are probably starting to appreciate that there are far more reasons for getting out of the market than there are for getting in. Unfortunately, most people are preoccupied with picking winning stocks and therefore lack a true appreciation of what constitutes a successful growth portfolio management system. Anyway, let's move on to the fun bit—taking profit.

Taking profit

As mentioned in the previous chapter, our strategy entails buying shares that will rise in price, some quite considerably, and then fall back by at least 20 per cent before we sell them. While this is an inherent property of our strategy, we can employ a very robust profit-taking benchmark in order to periodically grab some profits before they might slip away. I use the word *robust* because we'll find that if we pounce on our shares every time they rise in price, then we will suffer unwanted instability. But the rapid growth in the real-world example of Aristocrat Leisure Ltd (see figure 5.3), makes it an obvious target for profit taking.

Figure 5.3: Aristocrat Leisure Ltd

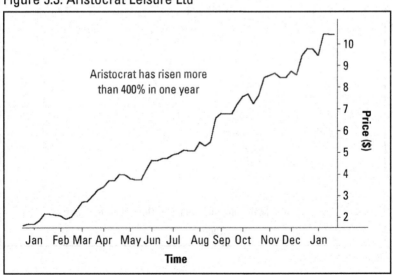

Source: MetaStock.

So the trick in this case is to set a very high profit-target level, and also make it proportional to the performance of the rest of our portfolio. It needs to be a relative measurement because we wouldn't want to take profit from our shares if they were all collectively going up together in sympathy with a strong rising market. So rather than take profit when a share price rises by at least 50 per cent from our purchase price, we will take profit when the share represents 15 per cent or more of the value of our entire portfolio; that is, when it's risen from 10 per cent of total capital to 15 per cent of total capital.

We will take enough profit to put the share back to its original portfolio weighting of 10 per cent. This will have the welcome side-effect of keeping our portfolio weightings fairly evenly trimmed. Assuming we bought Aristocrat at $3.00 in March and the rest of our portfolio's performance was flat for the relevant period, then the Aristocrat chart in figure 5.4 shows when we would have taken profit by selling one-third of the total position on each of three separate occasions.

Figure 5.4: Aristocrat Leisure Ltd — entry and profit-taking points

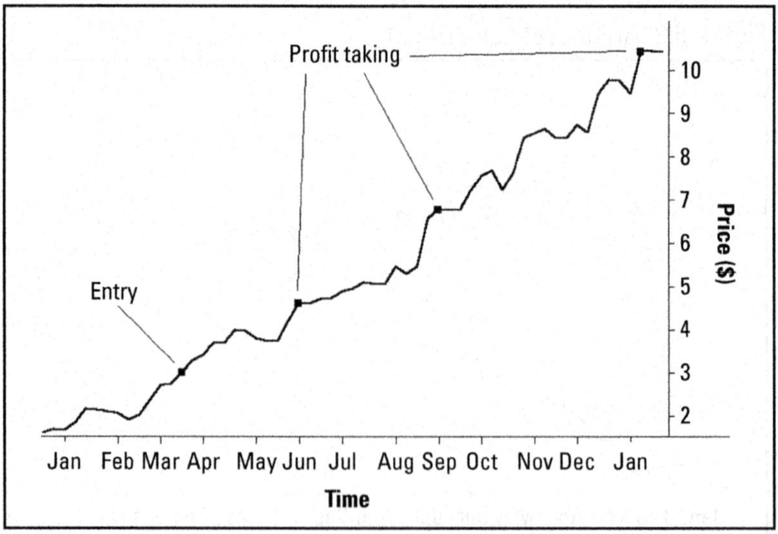

Source: MetaStock.

Given that we bought Aristocrat at $3.00 and its share price reached a high of $10.50, waiting until the share price fell by 20 per cent before selling it would have meant giving back $2.10 to the market, which represents 70 per cent of our original buy price of $3.00 — proceeds that we don't want to give back to the market so easily. So our profit-taking benchmark joins the list of exit criteria:

> *Profit-take sell: if a stock's portfolio weighting reaches 15 per cent of total capital then sell it down to restore the portfolio weighting of 10 per cent of total capital.*

Other considerations

We have now finished compiling all of the mandatory rules for selling our shares. Whenever we sell a position, we replace it with the fastest rising stock available that conforms with all the entry criteria discussed in chapter 4. Note that when buying shares we have to satisfy all the entry criteria at once, whereas a share must be sold if *any* of the sell conditions are met. This reinforces my earlier remark that managing our existing holdings is a far more demanding exercise than buying them in the first place. There are some other tasks we need to look at performing as well.

Taking cash

Unfortunately we don't get to take profits all the time, as very few of the shares we own will be as obliging as Aristocrat. But that doesn't mean we can afford to go without money, as the whole purpose of the exercise of investing is to supply ourselves with an income stream that will support a lifestyle of our choice. There will be times when we need to sell down our shares in order to take cash out to live on.

Taking cash can essentially be done at any time but it does require a moderate amount of common sense. Obviously it is not sensible to sell off shares in dribs and drabs, as this can seriously inflate the cost of brokerage. Your stockbroker will certainly be happy but it would be far more sensible and cheaper to do some relatively simple budgeting so you execute as few transactions as possible. In other words, work out how much money you need to live on for the next six months and then take enough cash from your portfolio to cover the entire period.

Deciding which shares to sell down, and by how much, starts with a relatively simple computation to work out what our total capital will be after we've taken our cash out of the equation. We can then calculate what 10 per cent of our new total capital will be and this will indicate to us which shares to trim back and by how much. The best way to illustrate how we do this task is with a working example.

Let's assume that the total value of all our open positions is $800 000 and we want to take out $50 000 to live on for the next six months, as we're planning to go on an overseas holiday.

- Our total capital after we take cash will be $800 000 – $50 000: $750 000

- Therefore, 10 per cent of our new total capital will be 10 per cent of $750 000: $75 000

Table 5.1 shows our portfolio before we've taken out our cash (total capital = $800 000).

Table 5.1: portfolio values before profit-taking

Share	Value
ABC	$75 000
EFG	$78 000
HIJ	$83 000
KLM	$97 000
LGT	$75 000
MEQ	$90 000
NIO	$77 000
NOP	$70 000
QRS	$73 000
TUV	$82 000

Given that our anticipated portfolio weighting per stock will be $75 000, we can commence selling back our shares to this level by starting with the largest positions first. Our approach to taking cash out of our portfolio is represented in table 5.2 (total capital is now $750 000).

Table 5.2: portfolio values and profit-taking sales

Share	Value	Sale
ABC	$75000	
EFG	$78000	
HIJ	$83000	3rd sale → sell $8000 worth of HIJ
KLM	$97000	1st sale → sell $22000 worth of KLM
LGT	$75000	
MEQ	$90000	2nd sale → sell $15000 worth of MEQ
NIO	$77000	
NOP	$70000	
QRS	$73000	
TUV	$82000	4th sale → sell $5000 worth of TUV

The result is that we will have taken a total of $50000 cash from our blue chip shares and have improved the overall balance of our portfolio weightings into the bargain. Now let's look at the flipside of this exercise — how to inject cash.

Injecting cash

Conveniently, this exercise is the exact reverse of taking cash. First, determine what your new total capital will be after you introduce your additional capital. Then, starting with the lowest positions first, build up each share to 10 per cent of your new total capital. The only additional caveat I would add in this instance is that I wouldn't bother spending any amount less than 5 per cent of my current total capital. I would deposit these small amounts in the bank until the balance represented at least 5 per cent of total capital before I bothered to inject it into the market.

Optimisation

Optimising a share portfolio is the process of reviewing each of your positions to see whether they are meeting your performance expectations. If a particular stock isn't performing well, then you would sell the position in favour of a better performing growth stock.

You might simply decide that, while a position is satisfactory, there is an even better opportunity you would rather invest your money in.

If you've ever owned shares then you'll probably be familiar with the hollow feeling you can get when someone tells you how well their shares have done in the past week, and when you look at your own shares you find that you've gone nowhere. The grass is always greener on the other side of the fence and we often find ourselves fighting the urge to constantly tweak our portfolio by shifting our money onto the latest winners. Unfortunately this is an all too common pitfall for the novice investor, who can be easily seduced by the excitement of chasing the market.

Suddenly we've gone from being an investor to being a speculator, or even worse — a gambler. The reality is that there will always be stocks that are going up in price while ours aren't, and chasing these stocks will seriously erode the benefit of using any well thought-out management system. Furthermore, the practice of constantly shifting money from one stock to another will have a detrimental impact on our blue chip growth portfolio because of a phenomenon that mathematicians call *random effect*.

The validity of probable outcomes depends largely on the sample size under examination. For instance, we all know that the probable outcome of tossing a coin is a 50–50 balance between getting heads and getting tails. But this 50–50 balance will rarely equate to getting one head and one tail if we toss the coin just two times. Even when we toss a coin 10 times we will rarely see a 50–50 result of five heads and five tails. But if we toss it 10 000 times, then we will very likely generate a sample of data that closely approximates the 50–50 balance of 5000 heads and 5000 tails.

The same logic applies to the stock market, where short-term share price movements are largely random, and the science of probability works far better on long-term market behaviour. So if we constantly tweak our portfolios then we will derail our investment strategy by introducing random effect.

Figure 5.5 shows a real-world example of how a very fast-rising share price (Caltex) can go sideways for long periods of time, or even suddenly dip sharply downwards.

Figure 5.5: pullback in Caltex's share price, 2003–05

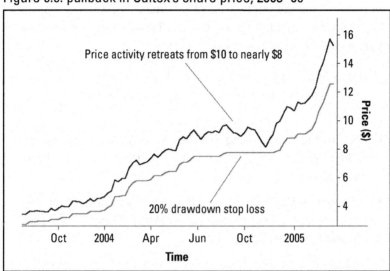

Price activity retreats from $10 to nearly $8

20% drawdown stop loss

Source: MetaStock.

If you jumped out of Caltex when its share price dipped to about $8, then you would have missed the subsequent rise in price to nearly $16. The price didn't breach our 20 per cent drawdown stop loss and it consistently maintained a very high rate of annual return throughout 2004. But imagine the temptation to jump ship to another stock when price activity started falling in late 2004.

The validity of probability calculations increase with any increase in sample size and the impact of randomisation increases with any reduction in sample size. So in order to allow the laws of probability a reasonable chance to work, I would suggest optimising your portfolio on an annual basis. Bear in mind, of course, that our strategy self-optimises anyway, and so periodic optimisation is unnecessary—but if you're like me, you probably can't resist.

The checklist

While I could continue to add more bells and whistles to our active funds management strategy, they would provide little if any benefit, but they would increase and unnecessarily add to our workload. So we can now present our final checklist, including both our reasons for buying and for selling. (Note that this list only includes mandatory actions and not optional ones.)

✓ *Curve-fit an SMA*. Adjust the period of a simple moving average so it sits just under slightly more than 12 months of price activity.

✓ *Measure the ROAR*. Using the SMA, measure the rate of annual return for every share in the S&P/ASX 200 index and prioritise them accordingly.

✓ *Set cut-off ROAR*. Determine the minimum acceptable rate of return by adding the break-even ROAR of 25 per cent to the current RBA cash rate target.

✓ *Measure liquidity*. Calculate 5 per cent of the average weekly turnover of each individual stock in terms of its cash flow (volume × average price).

✓ *Take the top 10*. Take the top 10 stocks from the list, ensuring that there are no more than four stocks from any particular industry and that the liquidity in terms of cash flow is acceptable in each case.

✓ *20 per cent drawdown stop loss*. Sell if the price activity draws down more than 20 per cent from the highest price in the past 12 months.

✓ *Moving average stop loss*. Sell if the share price drops below the 52-week SMA.

✓ *ROAR stop loss*. Sell if the rate of annual return falls below 25 per cent.

✓ *Top 40 stop loss*. Sell if a stock's ROAR falls outside the top 40.

✓ *Profit-take sell*. If a stock's portfolio weighting reaches 15 per cent of total capital then sell it down to a portfolio weighting of 10 per cent of total capital.

Now that we've completed designing the management system, it's time to test it out by applying it to some real shares. And for maximum convenience, I provide a weekly *Blue Chip Report* that contains all the information needed to execute this strategy. This report is extremely easy to use, and we will employ it in the next chapter when we take our trading system for a test drive.

But I'm not going to be the one doing the driving: Simon Sherwood, who helps me produce my weekly report, has kindly agreed to add his voice to this text. So I'll hand you over to Simon for the test drive and see you on the other side in part III, when we tackle the subject of seeking out and managing income stocks.

Chapter 6
Let's take a test drive

This chapter was written by Simon Sherwood, who assists with the production of my weekly report.

Now that Alan has fully explained the blue chip share trading strategy, we can step through the weekly process of managing your blue chip share growth portfolio to see how it works (in real time) and how much work we need to do to manage our growth shares.

In this chapter we will perform a share trading simulation using the blue chip investing strategy over a couple of months. To do this we are going to use the *Blue Chip Report* for all the share information that we will need and a simple spreadsheet, the ActVest Trade Recorder, to manage our portfolio. (If you subscribe to the weekly *Blue Chip Report* using the form at the end of this book, you will receive a complimentary copy of the ActVest Trade Recorder as a bonus.)

Our tools for the simulation

The *Blue Chip Report* is designed specifically for Alan's blue chip share trading strategy and provides all the information we need to implement the strategy. It takes away the hard work of our having to do the various searches, curve fitting, and so on, ourselves. Instead, we get a simple list of the shares that meet the specified criteria, as well as the information we need. Figure 6.1 (overleaf) shows a typical table of shares from the *Blue Chip Report*.

Figure 6.1: typical list of shares from the *Blue Chip Report*

	ASX200 Search Results				RBA Cash Rate Target = 4.75%	
Code	Company Name	Price($)	ROAR(%)	Cashflow($)	Industry Group	Stop Loss($)
LNC	Linc Energy	2.67	102.10	1267665	Energy	2.38
ILU	Iluka Resources	10.39	86.58	4480142	Materials	8.63
RIV	Riversdale Mining	15.52	71.19	5943768	Energy	13.60
MML	Medusa Mining	6.51	67.96	1436941	Materials	6.02
BLY	Boart Longyear	4.48	66.21	3419866	Capital Goods	3.88
MIN	Mineral Resources	11.58	59.65	1316770	Materials	10.78
PRU	Perseus Mining	2.90	57.53	1140529	Materials	2.70
MND	Monadelphous Group	20.66	56.39	1249735	Capital Goods	17.92
AWC	Alumina	2.22	50.44	10784795	Materials	2.09
WSA	Western Areas Mining	6.29	50.36	1098277	Materials	5.55
IPL	Incitec Pivot	4.20	50.21	9252161	Materials	3.70
OZL	OZ Minerals	1.48	45.03	7145529	Materials	1.42
FWD	Fleetwood Corp	11.40	44.95	475117	Automobile & Components	11.20
FMG	Fortescue Metals Group	5.88	43.01	20537882	Materials	5.50
SVW	Seven Network	8.33	42.75	519124	Media	7.31
WHC	Whitehaven Coal	6.47	39.97	1865668	Energy	5.72
RHC	Ramsay Health Care	18.46	39.08	1827447	Health Care	14.98
FLT	Flight Centre	22.00	34.88	1639193	Consumer Services	19.82
HDF	Hastings Div. Utilities Fund	1.51	34.44	280261	Utilities	1.36
ABC	Adelaide Brighton	3.24	28.97	1386673	Materials	2.91
IFL	IOOF Holdings	7.45	27.77	749344	Diversified Financials	6.40
IVC	Invocare	7.10	26.43	320207	Consumer Services	6.09
OSH	Oil Search	6.62	25.99	8390924	Oil Search	5.70

Each week a table like the one in figure 6.1 lists the top 40 shares in the S&P/ASX 200 according to their annual rate of return, providing it is greater than 25 per cent. There are times when there won't be 40 shares on the list. In fact, there are times, depending on what the market is doing, that there won't be any shares that meet the strategy's criteria. When this happens, it is definitely a good time not to be in the market! In the sample shown, we can see that there are more than 10 shares in the list. The report also shows the RBA cash rate, the current price, the cash flow, industry group and stop loss. We use this information to help with managing our portfolio, specifically liquidity, diversification and when to sell. The simulation in this chapter will demonstrate how this information is used.

Another component of the *Blue Chip Report* is Alan's market commentary. Each week Alan discusses the market to assist you with the implementation of the blue chip share trading strategy. This additional guidance is particularly useful when market sentiment is adversely affecting your decision making. Alan will often provide a market overview from a worldwide perspective and discuss how this affects the Australian market, as well as sometimes including specific details about the strategy. This can be anything like when not to be in the market or when it's time to start taking profits. It will make sure you keep up to date with what's happening in the market and how best to use the strategy. Figure 6.2 shows a sample of Alan's weekly commentary.

Figure 6.2: sample of Alan's weekly commentary from the *Blue Chip Report*

Not overly surprised and a little bit of investigation

While overseas markets started out the week on a positive note they have now turned down again and are, in most cases, looking set to retest their lows. And although I confess to being somewhat disappointed (as a sharp 'V' shaped reversal pattern would have been nice), I'm not overly surprised. As I pointed out last week, the U.S.'s SP-500 index has hit the brakes and we are still witnessing a <u>bottoming</u> action at this stage... but we are yet to witness a <u>reversal</u> pattern.

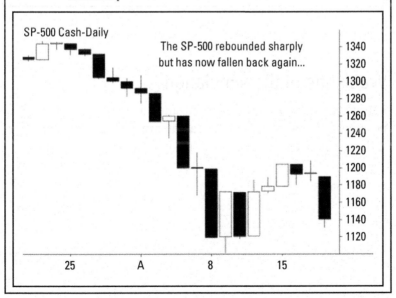

The trading ledger we will use in this simulation is a simple spreadsheet: the ActVest Trade Recorder. Using this spreadsheet isn't a compulsory part of the blue chip trading strategy, but it offers a simple way of monitoring your portfolio. In the simulation the ActVest Trade Recorder will keep track of all the information we need and it won't distract us with anything else. Figure 6.3 shows what the ActVest Trade Recorder (hereafter referred to as the Trade Recorder) looks like.

Figure 6.3: Trade Recorder spreadsheet with no data entered

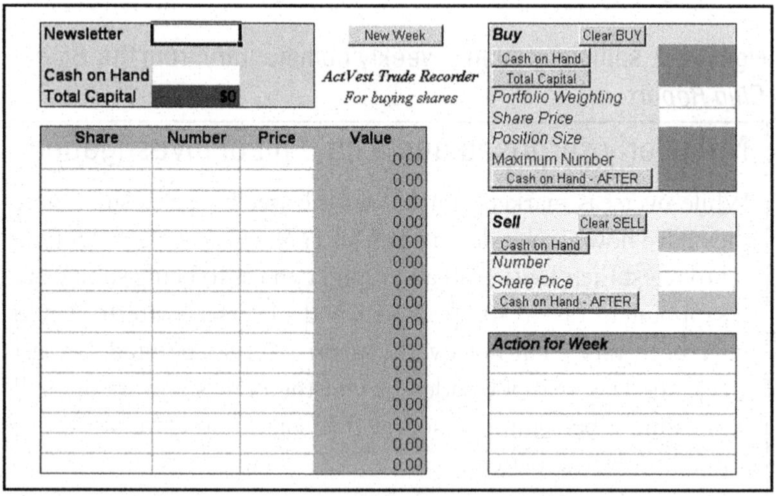

Now that we have the tools, let's get started on the simulation.

Week one of the simulation

We are going to start off with $1 million in cash and no open positions. This means our total capital available is also $1 million, and our Trade Recorder will look like figure 6.4.

Figure 6.4: Trade Recorder at the start of the simulation

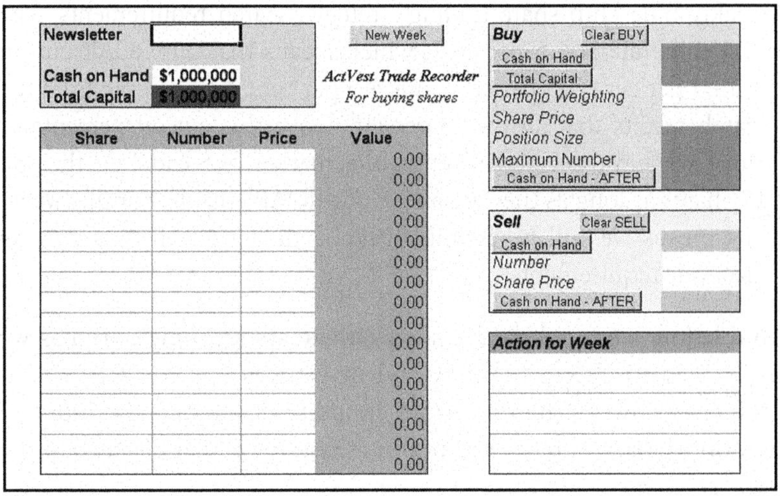

The simulation starts at the beginning of the 2010 financial year, 1 July 2010. The *Blue Chip Report* is published at the end of each week, and the first issue for the financial year in question is the issue for the week ending 2 July 2010.

Normally the first thing to do when looking at the *Blue Chip Report* is to read Alan's market commentary. However, for the sake of this exercise, we are going to ignore the additional guidance in the commentary and proceed straight to the search results. Let's have a look at the search results, shown in figure 6.5.

Figure 6.5: S&P/ASX 200 search results, week ending 2 July 2010

ASX200 Search Results				RBA Cash Rate Target = 4.50%	
Code	Company Name	Price($)	ROAR(%)	Cashflow($)	Industry Group	Stop Loss($)
BKN	Bradken	7.17	64.63	1572069	Capital Goods	6.38
SEK	Seek	7.08	63.58	3274612	Commercial Services & Supplies	6.71
IFL	IOOF Holdings	6.06	50.39	1052632	Diversified Financials	5.76
KCN	Kingsgate Consolidated	9.55	47.52	1126203	Materials	8.40
FWD	Fleetwood Corp	9.20	45.79	371449	Automobile & Components	7.84
ORI	Orica	24.66	39.39	8117319	Materials	22.00
WES	Wesfarmers	28.13	37.85	46393444	Capital Goods	26.17
TRS	The Reject Shop	15.65	33.09	407642	Retailing	13.53
IRE	Iress Market Technology	8.52	32.04	826010	Software & Services	7.28
RHC	Ramsay Health Care	13.75	30.53	2143647	Health Care	11.94

The ASX 200 search results show that 10 shares have passed the weekly blue chip share trading strategy's search requirements. The RBA cash rate is 4.5 per cent, which means that our ROAR cut-off is 29.5 per cent (25 per cent plus 4.5 per cent): we can see from the search results that all the shares are above this cut-off percentage. Once we have decided to enter the market, we can buy the top 10 shares as long as they are above our ROAR cut-off. For this week, that means we will be buying all the shares on the list, as they all meet our requirements.

But before we purchase the shares, there are a couple of things we still need to check: liquidity and diversification. We will look at the cash-flow ($) figure for our liquidity check and the industry group to make sure we are not purchasing too many shares in the one sector.

The cash-flow value represents 5 per cent of the average weekly turnover (in dollars) for that particular share. If we look at Bradken, for example, the cash-flow figure is $1 572 069—this is 5 per cent of Bradken's weekly turnover (on the sharemarket) and means that its weekly turnover (share price multiplied by volume) would in fact be just under $31.5 million! We need to make sure that our allocation for that position does not exceed the 5 per cent figure. In this case, that is quite acceptable, as we will be allocating only $100 000 to each position, which is 10 per cent of our total capital. This is well under the cash-flow figure for Bradken and as we look down the list we can see that all the shares have adequate liquidity for the amount we will be allocating per position.

Next we need to make sure that there are no more than four shares from any one industry group, and in this case the shares are well spread, as shown in table 6.1.

Table 6.1: industry groups for the shares shown in figure 6.5

Industry group	Number of companies
Automobile & Components	1
Capital Goods	2
Commercial Services & Supplies	1
Diversified Financials	1
Health Care	1
Materials	2
Retailing	1
Software & Services	1
Total	**10**

While it's highly unlikely to be a problem, it also pays to check that each share's entry price is above the stop loss value—and they all are. In this simulation we are restricted to using the closing price values listed in the *Blue Chip Report*. In real life you would need to make sure that the entry price when you place the order, presumably on Monday morning, is above the stop loss value.

It's time now to get on with buying the shares. We are allocating 10 per cent of our total capital to each position; that is, 10 per cent of $1 million, which is $100 000. And although the calculations are straightforward, we will still use the Trade Recorder to work out how many shares to buy.

To do this we use the Buy Calculator section of the Trade Recorder. Click on the Cash on Hand and Total Capital buttons, which will bring across the respective values, in this case $1 million for both. Then we enter the Portfolio Weighting = 10% and the Share Price = $7.17. The Trade Recorder then calculates the position size, the number of shares and the cash on hand after allowing for this purchase. Figure 6.6 (overleaf) shows what the Buy Calculator looks like after we have entered the relevant data.

Figure 6.6: Buy Calculator data for buying Bradken shares

Buy	Clear BUY	
Cash on Hand		1,000,000
Total Capital		1,000,000
Portfolio Weighting		10
Share Price		7.17
Position Size		100,000
Maximum Number		13,947
Cash on Hand - AFTER		900,000

The Buy Calculator tells us that we can buy 13 941 shares of Bradken at $7.17 with our $100 000. An important step now is to click on the Cash on Hand—AFTER button to update our cash-on-hand value, and we can click on the Clear BUY button to clear the Buy Calculator. Now our Trade Recorder looks like figure 6.7.

Figure 6.7: Trade Recorder after buying Bradken, updating cash on hand and clearing Buy Calculator

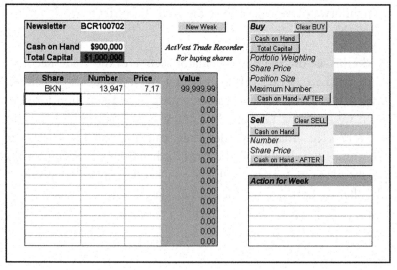

In real life, if you were using a full service broker, you would not need to do any calculations, as you would simply instruct them to purchase $100000 worth of Bradken. The broker would then confirm the final purchase price and number of shares.

In the Newsletter field we've entered the reference of the current week's *Blue Chip Report*. In this case it is BCR100702, which is in effect a date stamp (coded as BCR YY MM DD). After repeating the process another nine times, for all 10 companies, our Trade Recorder now looks like figure 6.8.

Figure 6.8: Trade Recorder after share purchases in all 10 companies recorded

Newsletter	BCR100702			New Week	Buy	Clear BUY
					Cash on Hand	
Cash on Hand	$61		*ActVest Trade Recorder*		Total Capital	
Total Capital	$999,995		*For buying shares*		Portfolio Weighting	
					Share Price	
Share	Number	Price	Value		Position Size	
BKN	13,947	7.17	99,999.99		Maximum Number	
SEK	14,124	7.08	99,997.92		Cash on Hand - AFTER	
IFL	16,501	6.06	99,996.06			
KCN	10,471	9.55	99,998.05		Sell	Clear SELL
FWD	10,869	9.20	99,994.80		Cash on Hand	
ORI	4,055	24.66	99,996.30		Number	
WES	3,554	28.13	99,974.02		Share Price	
TRS	6,389	15.65	99,987.85		Cash on Hand - AFTER	
IRE	11,737	8.52	99,999.24			
RHC	7,272	13.75	99,990.00		Action for Week	
			0.00			
			0.00			
			0.00			
			0.00			
			0.00			
			0.00			

We can see all 10 positions listed, the number and the purchase price and the value, which is roughly $100000 per position. As we can't buy fractions of shares, it's not always possible to purchase the exact dollar amount we require. In these cases we can err on the side of caution and purchase just under the amount. There will also be some minor rounding off in the various calculations, which will explain why the Total Capital field is not showing exactly $1 million.

After our first week, we have purchased our 10 shares and all our money is committed to the market. At this point we can click the New Week button on the Trade Recorder and this will save a copy of our spreadsheet (under the filename BCR100702.xls) for future reference and present us with the basic information we need to carry on with—and our portfolio has been sorted alphabetically (see figure 6.9)! Any time you want to click on the New Week button to save the spreadsheet, you must make sure that you have entered a Newsletter reference.

Figure 6.9: Trade Recorder after clicking the New Week button

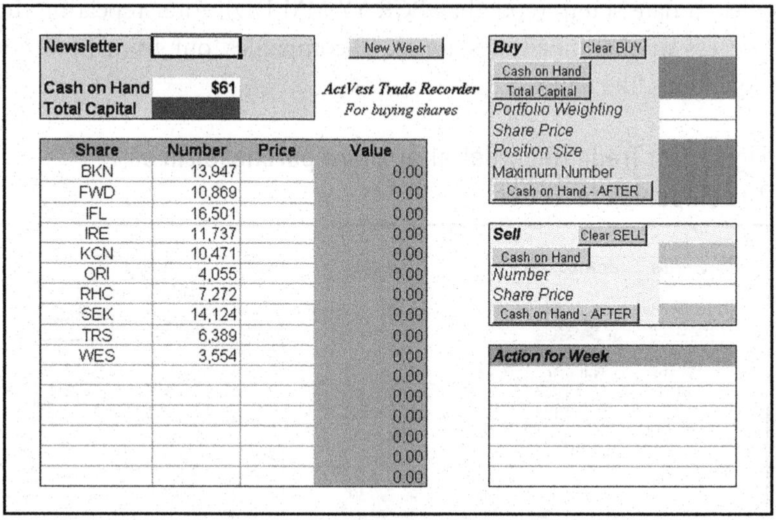

Week two

One thing we have to do this week, which we couldn't do last week, is to check our stop losses for all our open positions. Luckily the *Blue Chip Report* simplifies the checking process: all we need to do is make sure the share is still on the list, and that the closing price is above the listed stop loss value. If a share triggers any of the stop loss conditions (as explained by Alan in previous chapters), then the share fails the weekly search criteria and will no longer appear on the list. In these cases, the share should be sold and then replaced with a suitable candidate that meets the entry criteria (liquidity, diversification, and so on).

To see if we have to do anything this week, we'll look at the *Blue Chip Report* for the week ending 9 July 2010 (see figure 6.10).

Figure 6.10: S&P/ASX 200 search results, week ending 9 July 2010

ASX200 Search Results				RBA Cash Rate Target = 4.50%	
Code	Company Name	Price($)	ROAR(%)	Cashflow($)	Industry Group	Stop Loss($)
BKN	Bradken	7.41	63.68	1554635	Capital Goods	6.38
SEK	Seek	7.11	62.41	3268931	Commercial Services & Supplies	6.71
IFL	IOOF Holdings	6.46	49.38	1045291	Diversified Financials	5.76
KCN	Kingsgate Consolidated	9.55	45.80	1118911	Materials	8.40
FWD	Fleetwood Corp	9.53	44.62	380281	Automobile & Components	7.84
ORI	Orica	25.68	38.27	8317014	Materials	22.00
WES	Wesfarmers	28.46	36.63	46110352	Capital Goods	26.17
TRS	The Reject Shop	16.12	32.87	403361	Retailing	13.53
RHC	Ramsay Health Care	13.84	31.16	2128102	Health Care	11.94
IRE	Iress Market Technology	8.40	30.72	833908	Software & Services	7.28

All our shares are still there and they are all above the listed stop loss values, so we don't have to take any action this week. You will notice that the prices have changed and, in fact, a couple of shares have swapped places, but as long as they are still showing up in the search results, they haven't triggered an exit condition.

We won't do this each week but, for this week, we'll update our Trade Recorder with the current share prices, just to see what has happened. Often this is *not* a good idea, particularly if our emotions are linked directly to variations in the value of our portfolio. In reality, we only need to value our portfolio when we want to purchase a share or do general housekeeping.

One thing we do need to make sure of, though, is that no one position is greater than 15 per cent of our total capital. If this does happen, we would need to trim the position so it is equal to or less than 15 per cent of our total capital.

Figure 6.11 (overleaf) shows our Trade Recorder after we have entered the share prices from the *Blue Chip Report* for the week ending 9 July 2010.

Figure 6.11: Trade Recorder with share prices from the *Blue Chip Report,* week ending 9 July 2010

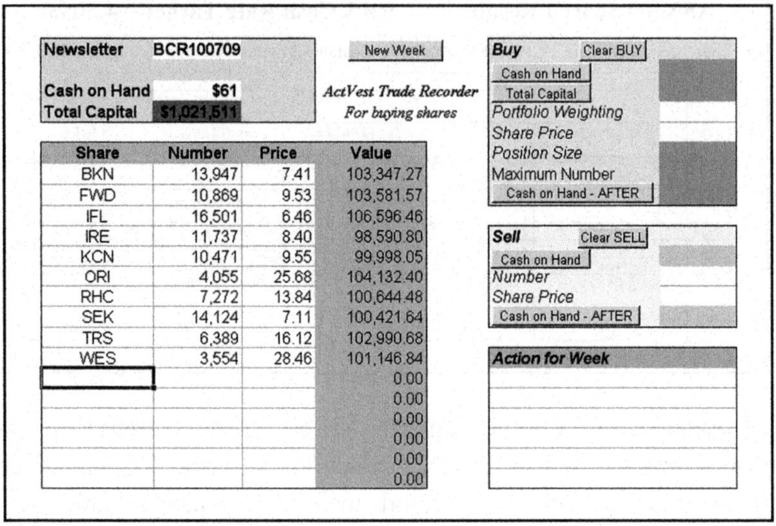

Newsletter	BCR100709			New Week	Buy	Clear BUY
					Cash on Hand	
Cash on Hand	$61		*ActVest Trade Recorder*		Total Capital	
Total Capital	$1,021,511		*For buying shares*		Portfolio Weighting	
					Share Price	
Share	**Number**	**Price**	**Value**		Position Size	
BKN	13,947	7.41	103,347.27		Maximum Number	
FWD	10,869	9.53	103,581.57		Cash on Hand - AFTER	
IFL	16,501	6.46	106,596.46			
IRE	11,737	8.40	98,590.80		Sell	Clear SELL
KCN	10,471	9.55	99,998.05		Cash on Hand	
ORI	4,055	25.68	104,132.40		Number	
RHC	7,272	13.84	100,644.48		Share Price	
SEK	14,124	7.11	100,421.64		Cash on Hand - AFTER	
TRS	6,389	16.12	102,990.68			
WES	3,554	28.46	101,146.84		**Action for Week**	
			0.00			
			0.00			
			0.00			
			0.00			
			0.00			
			0.00			

Some have gone up and some have gone down—a typical week of share trading! If we click the New Week button now, the spreadsheet will be saved under the filename BCR100709.xls. Note that we only have to save spreadsheets when we actually purchase or sell; saving portfolio valuations like this one is optional.

Week three

Along with checking our stop losses each week, we would normally read Alan's commentary to see if there is anything that we should take into account for that particular week. However, as stated earlier, for the sake of this simulation we are ignoring Alan's commentary.

Let's look at the S&P/ASX 200 (ASX200) search results from this week's *Blue Chip Report* (see figure 6.12).

Figure 6.12: ASX200 search results from the *Blue Chip Report,* week ending 16 July 2010

ASX200 Search Results				RBA Cash Rate Target = 4.50%	
Code	Company Name	Price($)	ROAR(%)	Cashflow($)	Industry Group	Stop Loss($)
BKN	Bradken	7.66	62.96	1607190	Capital Goods	6.38
SEK	Seek	7.19	61.48	3147381	Commercial Services & Supplies	6.71
IFL	IOOF Holdings	6.42	48.58	1014334	Diversified Financials	5.76
KCN	Kingsgate Consolidated	9.57	43.91	1080971	Materials	8.40
FWD	Fleetwood Corp	9.71	43.39	383642	Automobile & Components	7.94
ORI	Orica	24.93	37.06	8462004	Materials	22.00
TRS	The Reject Shop	15.76	32.78	376030	Retailing	13.53
RHC	Ramsay Health Care	13.81	31.88	2085298	Health Care	11.94
IRE	Iress Market Technology	8.55	29.37	768439	Software & Services	7.28

The prices of all the shares are above their stop losses and all the ones that appear on the list have obviously passed the search criteria: however, only nine shares are listed! As Wesfarmers (WES) no longer appears on the list, we know that it has not passed the weekly search criteria and therefore it has triggered an exit condition, so we have to sell it. For this exercise, we will use the previous week's closing price listed in the *Blue Chip Report,* which was $28.46. Once we have sold WES, we won't be able to replace it straightaway, as no other shares have passed the search criteria.

Using the Sell Calculator in the Trade Recorder, the first step is to click on the Cash on Hand button to bring across the cash on hand value. Next we enter in the number of shares and the share price. The calculator then works out how much cash we have on hand after the sale of this particular share. Again, we need to click on the Cash on Hand—AFTER button to update our cash-on-hand value.

First, we'll look at what the Sell Calculator looks like once we've entered the appropriate data (see figure 6.13).

Figure 6.13: Sell Calculator with data for sale of WES

Sell	Clear SELL	
Cash on Hand		61
Number		3554
Share Price		28.46
Cash on Hand - AFTER		**101,208**

And now we can look at the Trade Recorder after we've deleted WES and cleared the Sell Calculator (see figure 6.14).

Figure 6.14: Trade Recorder after the sale of WES

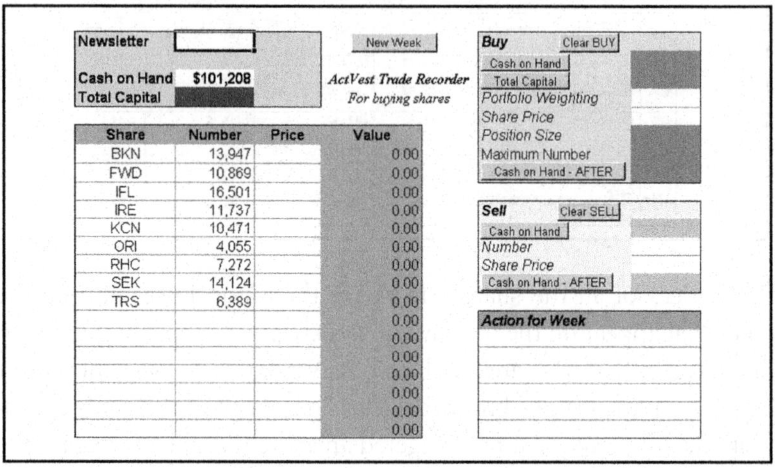

Share	Number	Price	Value
BKN	13,947		0.00
FWD	10,869		0.00
IFL	16,501		0.00
IRE	11,737		0.00
KCN	10,471		0.00
ORI	4,055		0.00
RHC	7,272		0.00
SEK	14,124		0.00
TRS	6,389		0.00

As we are unable to replace WES this week, there's no need to value the portfolio so, after clicking the New Week button (once we've entered the newsletter reference of course), it's time to move on.

Week four

Again, we're going to ignore Alan's commentary and go straight to the S&P/ASX 200 (ASX200) search results (see figure 6.15).

Figure 6.15: S&P/ASX 200 search results from the *Blue Chip Report,* week ending 23 July 2010

	ASX200 Search Results			RBA Cash Rate Target = 4.50%		
Code	Company Name	Price($)	ROAR(%)	Cashflow($)	Industry Group	Stop Loss($)
BKN	Bradken	7.93	62.52	1648643	Capital Goods	6.38
SEK	Seek	7.36	60.74	3022887	Commercial Services & Supplies	6.71
IFL	IOOF Holdings	6.56	47.80	988071	Diversified Financials	5.76
FWD	Fleetwood Corp	10.05	42.93	375147	Automobile & Components	8.04
KCN	Kingsgate Consolidated	9.73	42.50	1070908	Materials	8.40
ORI	Orica	25.42	36.05	8335529	Materials	22.00
RHC	Ramsay Health Care	14.75	32.96	2157509	Health Care	11.94
TRS	The Reject Shop	16.05	32.83	364198	Retailing	13.53
CMJ	Consolidated Media Holdings	3.14	32.22	1618645	Media	2.68
IRE	Iress Market Technology	8.20	28.45	770473	Software & Services	7.28

All of our nine companies still appear in the search results, so they've all passed the search criteria and they are all above their respective stop loss values. But you'll also notice that there is a new share on the list, Consolidated Media Holdings (CMJ), so we can top up our portfolio this week, replacing WES.

Doing a quick check of CMJ, we can see that it is above our entry ROAR cut-off (29.5 per cent); it has acceptable liquidity (the 5 per cent cash flow is more than $1.5 million and our 10 per cent allocation should be well below that); we currently don't have any shares in the Media Industry group; and it is above the stop loss value.

To buy CMJ we will again use the Buy Calculator section of the Trade Recorder and, as we need to work out our total capital, we'll have to enter in the share prices for our open positions. We need to do this because we have to know what our current total capital is in order to work out what 10 per cent of it will be. Figure 6.16 shows what the Trade Recorder looks like after we entered in the respective share values ready to purchase CMJ.

Figure 6.16: Trade Recorder showing values of open positions, week ending 23 July 2010

Newsletter	BCR100723			New Week		Buy	Clear BUY
						Cash on Hand	
Cash on Hand	$101,208			ActVest Trade Recorder		Total Capital	
Total Capital	$1,044,250			For buying shares		Portfolio Weighting	
						Share Price	
Share	Number	Price	Value			Position Size	
BKN	13,947	7.93	110,599.71			Maximum Number	
FWD	10,869	10.05	109,233.45			Cash on Hand - AFTER	
IFL	16,501	6.56	108,246.56				
IRE	11,737	8.20	96,243.40			Sell	Clear SELL
KCN	10,471	9.73	101,882.83			Cash on Hand	
ORI	4,055	25.42	103,078.10			Number	
RHC	7,272	14.75	107,262.00			Share Price	
SEK	14,124	7.36	103,952.64			Cash on Hand - AFTER	
TRS	6,389	16.05	102,543.45				
			0.00			Action for Week	
			0.00				
			0.00				
			0.00				
			0.00				
			0.00				
			0.00				

Using the Buy Calculator we click on the Cash on Hand and Total Capital buttons, enter the Portfolio Weighting of 10 per cent and the Share

Price of $3.14. The calculator then works out the Maximum Number of shares we can purchase, and we can enter this into the list of shares, complete with the share price so we can see our now full portfolio.

Let's have a look at the Trade Recorder showing our current portfolio and the figures used in the Buy Calculator, after we have clicked on the Cash on Hand—AFTER button to update the cash-on-hand figure (see figure 6.17).

Figure 6.17: Trade Recorder showing current open positions and Buy Calculator

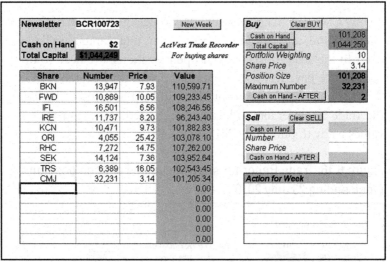

To finish the week, we'll clear the Buy Calculator and click New Week to save the spreadsheet and carry forward our open positions.

Jumping ahead to week eight

We've checked the *Blue Chip Report* for 30 July, and for 6 and 13 August, and nothing has really happened, so we haven't had to make changes to our Trade Recorder. Certainly all of our shares are still showing in the search results and they are all still above their stop loss value, so now it's on to the week ending 20 August. Ignoring Alan's commentary (which we are doing *only* because this is a simulation—in real life, it would be the first thing we would read!), we can check the S&P/ASX 200(ASX200) search results (see figure 6.18).

Figure 6.18: S&P/ASX 200 search results from the *Blue Chip Report,* week ending 20 August 2010

ASX200 Search Results				RBA Cash Rate Target = 4.50%		
Code	Company Name	Price($)	ROAR(%)	Cashflow($)	Industry Group	Stop Loss($)
BKN	Bradken	7.54	59.01	1433321	Capital Goods	6.38
RIV	Riversdale Mining	9.18	58.83	2070260	Energy	8.88
CEY	Centennial Coal Company	6.03	58.64	9142301	Energy	4.83
SEK	Seek	7.60	57.77	2317341	Commercial Services & Supplies	6.71
IFL	IOOF Holdings	6.45	46.37	842248	Diversified Financials	5.76
HDF	Hastings Div. Utilities Fund	1.37	42.74	304553	Utilities	1.11
FWD	Fleetwood Corp	9.72	40.23	335712	Automobile & Components	8.04
KCN	Kingsgate Consolidated	9.81	37.79	1053960	Materials	8.40
ANN	Ansell	12.76	36.60	2125065	Health Care	10.87
RHC	Ramsay Health Care	13.92	36.33	1831625	Health Care	11.94
ORI	Orica	25.21	31.82	7330602	Materials	22.00
TRS	The Reject Shop	16.12	31.81	327080	Retailing	13.53
AMC	Amcor	6.52	30.10	8147146	Materials	5.47
CMJ	Consolidated Media Holdings	3.23	28.76	1481396	Media	2.68
COH	Cochlear	68.88	28.27	5748031	Health Care	62.08
SEV	Seven Network	7.41	25.93	0	Media	6.40

Checking our open positions, we can see that they are all there except IRE, which has obviously failed the search criteria and therefore has to be sold. We'll follow the same process as before, using the Sell Calculator and the previous week's closing price. After the sale our Trade Recorder, complete with Sell Calculator, looks like figure 6.19, with IRE deleted.

Figure 6.19: Trade Recorder showing open positions and portfolio after the sale of IRE

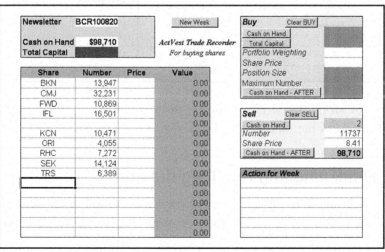

Now, as we have some cash on hand and only nine positions, we can replace IRE with the next highest share on the list. Looking down the list we can see the next suitable candidate is Centennial Coal (CEY). CEY meets all our entry criteria (ROAR cut-off, liquidity, diversification, and so on.) so we will go ahead and purchase CEY using the Buy Calculator and then update our Trade Recorder accordingly.

The process is the same as that used earlier: we need to enter the share prices for our open positions so we can calculate our total capital, use the Buy Calculator to work out the number of CEY shares to purchase and then add CEY to our portfolio. Figure 6.20 shows the Trade Recorder after completing the purchase of CEY (the Buy Calculator hasn't been cleared so you can see the values used).

Figure 6.20: Trade Recorder showing the portfolio after the purchase of CEY before Buy Calculator is cleared

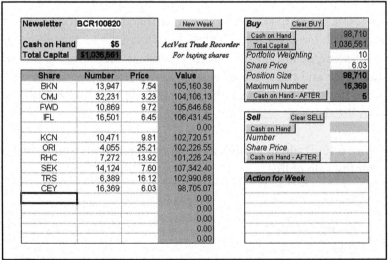

To finish off this week, we'll clear the Buy Calculator and click the New Week button to save the spreadsheet.

Week nine and reaching the end

This brings us to the end of August, which is probably as good a time as any to stop the simulation, as it means we have been effectively trading for two months. As usual we'll check the ASX200 search results (see figure 6.21).

Figure 6.21: S&P/ASX 200 search results from the *Blue Chip Report,* week ending 27 August 2010

	ASX200 Search Results			RBA Cash Rate Target = 4.50%		
Code	Company Name	Price($)	ROAR(%)	Cashflow($)	Industry Group	Stop Loss($)
CEY	Centennial Coal Company	6.02	59.18	9081141	Energy	4.83
RIV	Riversdale Mining	9.29	58.83	2191410	Energy	8.88
BKN	Bradken	7.20	57.05	1395516	Capital Goods	6.38
SEK	Seek	7.20	56.39	2290181	Commercial Services & Supplies	6.71
IFL	IOOF Holdings	6.42	45.39	792373	Diversified Financials	5.76
HDF	Hastings Div. Utilities Fund	1.31	42.18	297452	Utilities	1.11
FWD	Fleetwood Corp	9.87	39.41	330358	Automobile & Components	8.04
RHC	Ramsay Health Care	14.22	36.70	2063160	Health Care	11.94
KCN	Kingsgate Consolidated	9.65	36.67	1059409	Materials	8.40
ANN	Ansell	13.12	36.20	2123369	Health Care	10.87
TRS	The Reject Shop	16.48	31.13	320601	Retailing	13.53
ORI	Orica	25.04	30.17	7138863	Materials	22.00
AMC	Amcor	6.67	29.94	7861799	Materials	5.47
COH	Cochlear	68.43	27.98	5706486	Health Care	62.08
CMJ	Consolidated Media Holdings	3.26	27.67	1428899	Media	2.68

Checking the list, all our shares are there and all are above their respective stop loss values. To round things off, we will do a quick valuation of our portfolio using the closing prices from the *Blue Chip Report* for the week ending 27 August 2010 (see figure 6.22).

Figure 6.22: Trade Recorder showing the final value of portfolio using closing prices from the *Blue Chip Report,* week ending 27 August 2010

Newsletter	BCR100827			New Week		Buy	Clear BUY	
						Cash on Hand		
Cash on Hand		$5		ActVest Trade Recorder		Total Capital		
Total Capital		$1,030,226		For buying shares		Portfolio Weighting		
						Share Price		
Share	Number	Price	Value			Position Size		
BKN	13,947	7.20	100,418.40			Maximum Number		
CEY	16,369	6.02	98,541.38			Cash on Hand - AFTER		
CMJ	32,231	3.26	105,073.06					
FWD	10,869	9.87	107,277.03			Sell	Clear SELL	
IFL	16,501	6.42	105,936.42			Cash on Hand		
KCN	10,471	9.65	101,045.15			Number		
ORI	4,055	25.04	101,537.20			Share Price		
RHC	7,272	14.22	103,407.84			Cash on Hand - AFTER		
SEK	14,124	7.20	101,692.80					
TRS	6,389	16.48	105,290.72			Action for Week		
			0.00			End of simulation		
			0.00					
			0.00					
			0.00					
			0.00					
			0.00					

You can see that some shares went up, some went down and some did very little. This really is what we would expect to see after a couple of months and is typical of how the blue chip trading strategy works in real time.

That concludes our simulation of Alan's blue chip share trading strategy using the *Blue Chip Report*. Hopefully you'll now have a better idea of how the strategy works and also how easy the *Blue Chip Report* makes the whole process.

PART III

Managing a blue chip share income portfolio

Chapter 7

Introduction to income shares

By this stage you should be very familiar with what constitutes a growth stock, how to hunt them down and how to manage them. Now we're going to jump to the other side of the fence by investigating what constitutes an income stock or share, how to hunt them down and how to manage them.

An income stock is one that we buy and hold for the purpose of sharing in a company's profits rather than capitalising on the growth of its share price. To get our heads around this, we need to understand the difference between shares and the underlying companies that they represent. The difference is the crowd.

The crowd

The crowd is the market participants who collectively place a value on companies via their share price. That's you and me, by the way, and unfortunately, contrary to conventional economic theory, we aren't that efficient when it comes to valuing our assets. What this means is that the value of a company and the profits it generates aren't directly linked.

If 10 million shares are issued for Company D and the shares are trading at $2 each then the market capitalisation, or the value that the market places on the company, is:

$$10\,000\,000 \text{ shares} \times \$2 = \$20 \text{ million}$$

Now let's assume that there is no change in the trading conditions of the company other than some speculation about a foreign competitor entering the marketplace in the future. If the shares are sold down to $1 each, then the market has halved the value it places on Company D.

$$10\,000\,000 \text{ shares} \times \$1 = \$10 \text{ million}$$

The key point here is that the share price may alter substantially without any actual change in the performance of the underlying company. Supposedly, the value that market participants place on a company and the actual value of the company in terms of its assets and earnings should be pretty much one and the same — in theory.

But the crowd forms a slippery barrier between the value of the shares and what the company is actually worth. Furthermore, the crowd may value the shares using factors that have little or nothing to do with the company itself. While this may seem to be a complication, it is the very reason for the marketplace's existence. If we could value shares using just solid facts, then the stock market would probably cease to exist, as trading would dry up.

Items with a fixed value can't be traded in a marketplace. (You wouldn't pay $60 for a $50 note, for instance; nor would you sell a $50 note for $40.) Shares are an intangible representation of tangible companies. The two components are linked together through us, the crowd. But although we own public companies by possessing shares in them, it is important to differentiate between shares and the public companies they represent.

In figure 7.1 you can see how the crowd effectively devalued Australian public companies by 43 per cent during the stock market crash of 1987. This devaluation had virtually nothing to do with any change in the performance of Australian public companies, but had a lot to do with global investor sentiment at the time. In other words, the US stock market crashed and we followed.

Figure 7.1: All Ordinaries index, 1986–87, showing the 1987 crash

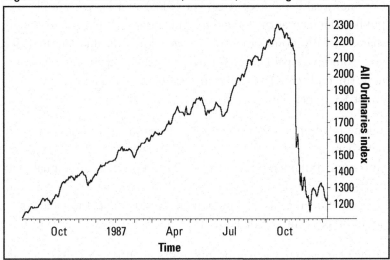

Source: MetaStock.

Dividend payments were largely unaffected and didn't fall by 43 per cent in October 1987. The collapse in the All Ordinaries during October 1987 was due to the sentiment of the crowd and had little to do with the earning capacity of Australian public companies.

Tangible assets

So there are Australian publicly listed companies, which are tangible in nature, and the shares that are traded on the Australian stock market that represent them, which are intangible. Now as an investor who wants to buy into the underlying business and share in its very real profits, I need to focus on the tangible business and try to ignore crowd sentiment.

If we are investing in companies for income, then our perception is that we own part of the company as a tangible asset. The purpose of our assets is to produce passive income, and companies produce this income for us by paying an annual dividend, which is a share or portion of the profits. We may also have the bonus of tax credits, if the company has already paid some or all of the tax owing on its profits, which are paid out to us as dividends.

Commonwealth Bank of Australia (CBA) is a good example of a public company as an income-producing asset. If you had bought shares in CBA around the time of their initial listing, late in 1991, you would have paid approximately $6.50 per share and you would now (in mid 2012) be receiving an annual dividend payment of about $3.25 per share.

Taking inflation into consideration, your initial investment of $6.50 per share is worth just over $15 in today's money. In real terms your annual dividend payment of $3.25 represents an annual yield of just over 20 per cent—not bad. And I haven't even taken into consideration the tax credits, which would bump the yield up to about 30 per cent, a little better than not bad.

I'll delve more into calculating and assessing income yields in chapter 10, but the point I want to make is that this is all independent of CBA's share price, which has gone nowhere of late. In fact, it's actually down on where it was four years ago, and so from a growth perspective it would be a terrible proposition (see figure 7.2).

Figure 7.2: CBA share price 2007–11

Source: MetaStock.

Key objectives of income investors

An income investor has little concern about the direction of share price movements. As an income investor you want to accumulate assets, not buy and sell them. Your key objectives are very different from an investor seeking growth:

- You want to own your income-producing assets forever—you never want to have to sell them.

- You must very carefully assess the income-producing capabilities of your assets.

- You must purchase your assets at the lowest price possible.

- Your assets must be able to withstand the passage of time.

Of course, Warren Buffett has the financial wherewithal to control the public companies that he buys, and we don't—so we must be very careful to choose companies that will last us a lifetime. You can see how this single criterion rules out high technology stocks, given the volatility of their operating environment. This is why Warren Buffett has a strong preference for companies in low-tech sectors that produce essential products, such as toilet paper manufacturers. Other examples of these are Coca-Cola and Gillette: Buffett believed that we all drink Coke and all men shave. He wasn't entirely correct here, but he wasn't far off the mark either, and these investments served both Warren Buffett and his company, Berkshire Hathaway, very well.

Asset-class shares

Companies like Coca-Cola and Gillette are in fact lifetime income-producing assets, which I will refer to from this point onwards as asset-class shares. Now, to seek out asset-class shares, we must first establish a set of specific benchmarks to work with. But you should understand from the outset that there are no right or wrong benchmarks, and the selection criteria we use are very much a matter of personal opinion.

While there is a degree of mystery surrounding the apparent genius of the likes of Warren Buffett and Ben Graham (Warren Buffett's mentor), they in their turn use or used a discrete set of pre-defined benchmarks to seek out asset class-shares—not a crystal ball.

Searching for income stocks or lifetime income-producing assets is a boring and monotonous task that is reliant on hard work, not an ability to foretell the future. That said, let's look at the guidelines for determining our benchmarks. As we are seeking lifetime income-producing assets, we must consider the following three areas:

- *Lifetime.* Asset-class shares represent companies that will exist for our lifetime. Ideally we never want to sell our income stocks, so they must last a lifetime.

- *Income.* Asset-class shares must have an acceptable, or better, dividend yield. We are acquiring asset-class shares for their income, not their capital growth.

- *Quality and value.* Asset-class shares should be of good quality and value, like anything that has to last a lifetime.

Before delving into each of these areas in detail, it is important to reiterate that each of us has a different set of financial circumstances and financial goals, and we are all different ages. Therefore, the guidelines and benchmarks offered here are not set in stone and should be tailored to your own needs and situation in life.

Lifetime

In order to make a judgement as to whether a company will last our lifetime, we must first quantify our own life expectancy and, second, determine the life expectancy of the publicly listed company in question. Human life expectancy is well beyond the scope of this discussion, so we will move on to the question of a company's lifetime expectancy.

There are several guidelines that we can combine in order to estimate a company's life expectancy. The main problem is that we have to make qualitative judgements about the stability of different commercial operating environments—we must make an assessment of the longevity and stability of different industry sectors.

Based on his choices, Warren Buffett believes we're all going to keep shaving long into the future and keep drinking fizzy drinks. However, Buffett completely abstained from the tech boom in the late 1990s for the simple reason that he perceived the operating environment to be subject to rapid change — a sensible assessment in my opinion. Time has shown that some technology companies have done extremely well, but many went the way of the dodo.

Another guideline we can consider is the size of a company in terms of its market capitalisation. The simple logic here is that the bigger a company is, the less likely it is to disappear off the face of the earth. Mind you, those who owned shares in HIH and Enron in the United States might disagree with this logic.

But while size doesn't necessarily ensure survival, it is a statistically valid factor, because the vast majority of delistings occur among companies with smaller capitalisation. For asset-class shares, I apply a cut-off of $100 million capitalisation as a minimum, as this level fairly accurately defines the top 500 shares listed on the ASX. I consider $50 million to $100 million to be mid cap and anything below $50 million to be small capitalisation companies.

We still need to assess each company on its own merits, as there are always individual circumstances that can't be incorporated into global benchmarks. A typical example of this would be ANZ or Westpac. These banks would become likely takeover targets by the larger banks in the event of the dismantling of the federal government's four pillar banking policy (which prevents our four largest banks from merging with each other, thus preserving a reasonable degree of competition in the banking sector). Therefore, the four pillar banking policy could have a direct effect on the life expectancy of these companies.

It would be a very similar scenario for media companies in the event of changes to the restrictions on foreign ownership of media assets in Australia. So when it comes to assessing the life expectancy of a company it will ultimately depend on personal judgement.

Income

Before we look at establishing a minimum benchmark for income, it is important to understand the inverse relationship between a company's share price and its dividend yield, which is the amount of income generated per share, per year, and expressed as a percentage. A company with a share price of $10 that pays an annual dividend of 50 cents is said to have a dividend yield of 5 per cent, which is 50 cents divided by $10, expressed as a percentage.

We can observe the inverse relationship between share price and dividend yield with the use of charts. Both charts for Blackmores (see figures 7.3 and 7.4) represent the same time period, but one chart is of the share price while the other is its dividend yield.

Figure 7.3: Blackmores—falling share price

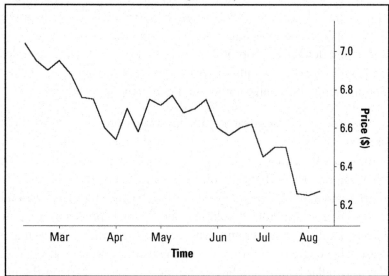

Source: MetaStock.

Blackmores' share price is steadily falling over time, while the dividend yield is steadily rising. (The dividend yield chart in figure 7.4 was generated using Stock Doctor <www.stockdoctor.com.au> by Lincoln Indicators, a proven fundamental analysis program, unique to Australia. I have been using the Stock Doctor program for more than a decade and I strongly recommend it.)

Figure 7.4: Blackmores — rising dividend yield

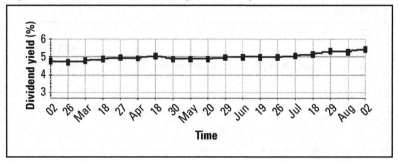

Source: StockDoctor.

As the average dividend yield of the entire stock market has a very strong tendency to track official interest rates, our expectations in terms of income must remain flexible and in keeping with the Reserve Bank of Australia's official target cash rate. As the average dividend yield is usually just *below* the official target cash rate, it would be prudent to set our minimum benchmark at the RBA's official rate, which can be found at <www.rba.gov.au>.

This will ensure that our income stream is always *above* the official cash rate and we're always ahead of the curve. What's more, this benchmark doesn't take into consideration any franking credits (tax credits) that we might also be entitled to.

Be aware that whatever benchmark we choose to employ is only our starting point, and it should reflect our tolerance towards *minimum* income. The plan is that, with the passage of time, the income streams from these assets will grow in magnitude and proportionality with respect to the prices we originally paid for them. If we apply the benchmark of 4.75 per cent (the RBA target cash rate at that particular time) to the dividend yield chart of Blackmores, we can see that it exceeds our expectations in terms of minimum income requirements (see figure 7.5, overleaf).

Figure 7.5: Blackmores — dividend yield exceeding RBA target cash rate

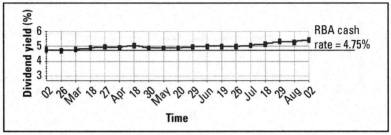

Source: StockDoctor.

But, taking the example of Blackmores a step further, the dilemma we now face is, 'Do we buy today, or, given that the share price is falling, do we wait for a possibly higher income yield in the future?' The answer is this: we buy if the current dividend yield is above our threshold, and we continue to accumulate shares into the future if the share price continues to fall. We will return to this area when we get into the subject of market timing in part IV.

Furthermore, when we are accumulating shares in a particular company, while the share price continues to fall we could in fact be losing money. In other words, if we add the dividend payments to our capital losses, the result is a negative one. But given our time frame of lifetime, these losses are just the short-term impact of an imperfect market entry.

In a final note on income, it is always wise to ensure that the dividend per share, or DPS, is not of an abnormal nature and is in keeping with the normal dividend payment pattern of the company. Check that the company has not paid out an extraordinarily large dividend because its income has been abnormally inflated due to a unique circumstance, such as the sale of a major asset.

An example of this is when Mayne Nickless sold its interest in Optus, which led to a bonus payment to shareholders of an extra $1 per share. With its share price around $6.00 at the time, you can imagine how this sent the dividend yield temporarily skyrocketing. Anyone who didn't look for abnormals in Mayne Nickless's balance sheet at that time wouldn't have realised the true cause of its high yield.

So you can see there are some pitfalls that we need to watch out for. As we are acquiring these shares specifically for the purpose of realising an income stream, we need to get the assessment of their income correct. We also need to make sure that we're buying into quality businesses and getting good value for our money when we do so, which is the next area of discussion.

Quality and value

Before we delve into what constitutes quality and value when it comes to asset-class shares, and how we seek out these attributes, we need to make a bit of a detour through the science of fundamental analysis. With income stocks we are buying into the underlying business, and to assess the quality of a business and its value, we have to employ fundamental analysis.

So it's best if we start with a general discussion on this topic first, and the best person to provide that discussion is Martin Roth, the widely acclaimed and best-selling author of the book series *Top Stocks*, published by Wrightbooks. I'll return in chapter 9, where we will begin the hunt for income stocks.

Chapter 8
Fundamental analysis

This chapter was written by Martin Roth, best-selling author of the book series *Top Stocks*.

There are a number of ways to analyse a company when you are deciding where to invest. One of these is fundamental analysis, which involves asking many questions about a company, such as:

- What does the company do?
- How does it make its money?
- Is it profitable?
- Is it growing?
- Is it financially sound?

Fundamental analysis also includes looking at the company's shares. For example: are they cheap or expensive in comparison with rival companies? Is the dividend yield high or low?

It's generally not difficult to find out what a company does, although you may be unaware of all the activities of some diverse corporations.

But it is also important to learn where companies make their profits. For instance, Wesfarmers is now best known for its retail interests — Coles,

Bunnings, Officeworks, Kmart and Target—which together make up more than 85 per cent of total company turnover. But it also has important interests in coalmining. While this provides a relatively small part of total revenues, in some years it has contributed more than a quarter of company profit.

Another example is BHP Billiton. Iron ore and petroleum make up a little more than 40 per cent of the company's sales revenues, but in the year to June 2011 they contributed 60 per cent of company profits. Clearly, fluctuations in iron ore and petroleum prices have an important bearing on profits for this company.

So it's more important to know how it makes its profits than what it does. You also need to assure yourself that those profits will continue. Without a flow of profits, a company will not be able to pay a dividend, and eventually even its survival could be in doubt.

Introducing ratios

A lot of company analysis is carried out by calculating ratios. This allows you to condense a large amount of complex information into an easily digestible and standardised form. Ratios allow you to make many comparisons—for instance, between different years for a single company, between companies of varying sizes, or between entire industries.

Some ratios are published regularly in the financial press or in stockbroker research reports, and you won't need to work them out yourself. For others, or to obtain raw financial data and calculate them yourself, you will need to obtain a copy of the company annual report—usually available on the company's own website or at the ASX website <www.asx.com.au> (look under Company Announcements).

If you want to analyse a company, you must become familiar with the main components of a company financial report, especially the income statement (also known as the profit and loss statement), the balance sheet and the cash flow statement.

The three kinds of ratios discussed in the rest of the chapter are profitability ratios, debt ratios and stock market ratios. All of these ratios are important, and different financial analysts will place a different degree of importance on each group.

Profitability ratios

The three main profitability ratios that investors should be familiar with are:

- earnings before interest and taxation (EBIT)
- EBIT margin
- return on equity.

Earnings before interest and taxation

In its annual report, each company presents a profit and loss statement, which is of great significance for analysts.

Newspaper reports of a company's profits usually focus on the after-tax figure, as it is this amount that theoretically is 'owned' by shareholders. But analysts often prefer another measure of profits: earnings before interest and taxation (EBIT). In other words, they take the pre-tax profit and to it add back the company's net interest payments (the interest it has to pay on its borrowings, minus the interest it receives on its cash in the bank).

There are two main reasons for preferring EBIT to the after-tax profit figure for analysis purposes. First, using a pre-tax figure eliminates discrepancies between various companies' tax rates. Second, companies use different methods of financing their operations: some use equity (capital raised by issuing shares, options, and so on), and some use bank debt. Adding interest payments to earnings helps to minimise these differences, which makes comparisons more valid.

The EBIT figure can be used in making year-on-year profit comparisons, and obviously a rising figure is to be preferred, though note that this could be as a result of higher borrowings leading to bigger interest payments.

Note too that you will also sometimes see an EBITDA figure, which is EBIT with the company's depreciation and amortisation amounts added back.

EBIT margin

This ratio tells you how much profit a company is making on its operations, expressed as a percentage. The formula is:

EBIT margin = (EBIT ÷ sales revenue) × 100

A rising EBIT margin—whether sales and profits are rising or falling—means the company is becoming more efficient. Its costs—salaries, raw materials, factory operations, and so on—are falling as a percentage of sales (although interest rate fluctuations can also influence the trend of this ratio).

Clearly a high EBIT margin is desirable, though many excellent firms do well with low margins. These are often companies like efficient retailers that have a high turnover.

The list of EBIT margin figures in table 8.1, for a sample of Australian companies, shows the wide variance that exists. (All figures are from the June 2011 accounts.) This selection of eight Australian companies will be used for all the tables that follow in this chapter.

Table 8.1: EBIT margin figures for a sample of Australian companies, June 2011

Company	EBIT margin
Australian Securities Exchange (ASX)	75.9%
Wotif.com Holdings	50.2%
BHP Billiton	44.3%
Computershare	24.8%
Tabcorp Holdings	20.2%
Harvey Norman Holdings	15.5%
Monadelphous Group	8.9%
Woolworths	6.1%

Return on equity

The return on equity ratio shows the after-tax profit as a percentage of shareholders' equity, which is part of the balance sheet, and is the amount left over when all the company's liabilities have been accounted for.

In other words, shareholders' equity is, in theory, what the shareholders would own if the company's assets were used to pay off liabilities. I say 'in theory', because there is no guarantee that all assets or liabilities would translate exactly into the values given in the balance sheet.

And, in theory, the after-tax profit is also an amount that is owned by shareholders. This ratio tells shareholders how much the company's managers made for them, on their investment. The formula is:

Return on equity = (after-tax profit ÷ shareholders' equity) × 100

The best companies will generally achieve a double-digit return on equity. However, this can be achieved by raising debt levels, so this ratio should be used in conjunction with others, to check the company's debt.

Nevertheless, some analysts believe the trend in return on equity is one of the best indicators of likely stock price performance. A high return on equity means the company has profits to fuel further growth, so look for a company whose return on equity is already quite high — at least in double digits — and growing year by year.

Table 8.2 shows the June 2011 return on equity figures for the eight selected companies.

Table 8.2: return-on-equity figures for the selected Australian companies, June 2011

Company	Return on equity
Wotif.com Holdings	58.4%
Monadelphous Group	56.3%
BHP Billiton	42.1%
Woolworths	28.0%
Tabcorp Holdings	23.2%
Computershare	21.6%
Australian Securities Exchange (ASX)	12.0%
Harvey Norman Holdings	11.7%

Debt ratios

A company's exposure to debt is a key risk factor that investors should always consider. Investors can use these two key debt ratios to assess debt:

- debt-to-equity ratio
- interest cover.

Debt-to-equity ratio

This ratio expresses debt as a percentage of shareholders' equity; it is one of many measures that help you understand a company's debt exposure.

There are several ways to calculate the ratio, but the easiest is simply to express all of a company's liabilities as a percentage of shareholders' equity. It is, however, more accurate to use debt on which interest must be paid, and also to deduct the company's cash holdings (on which it is receiving interest). That means you might see different debt-to-equity ratio figures for the same company in different sources, depending on the method of calculation. The formula is:

$$\text{Debt-to-equity ratio} = (\text{[borrowings} - \text{cash]} \div \text{shareholders' equity}) \times 100$$

The higher the figure, the greater the possibility that the company might one day experience difficulties in repaying its debts. This is a particular concern in an environment of rising interest rates.

There is no particular figure considered to be safe, although many analysts believe a company is in no danger as long as its debt-to-equity ratio does not exceed 100 per cent. However, conservative investors would be advised to investigate carefully before investing in any company with a ratio higher than 60 to 70 per cent.

Much also depends on surrounding circumstances. A company with stable profits and cash flow might be considered safer, even with high debt levels, than a company with volatile profits. Thus, Telstra, generally viewed as a safe investment (if not always a profitable one), in June 2011 had a debt-to-equity ratio of more than 90 per cent.

It is safer to operate on a higher debt-to-equity ratio when interest rates are low than when rates are high.

Table 8.3 shows debt-to-equity ratios for the selected Australian companies. Companies with a '0%' figure either have no borrowings or have cash holdings higher than the amount of their borrowings.

Table 8.3: debt-to-equity ratio for the selected Australian companies, June 2011

Company	Debt-to-equity ratio
Australian Securities Exchange (ASX)	0%
Monadelphous Group	0%
Wotif.com Holdings	0%
BHP Billiton	10.1%
Harvey Norman Holdings	21.9%
Woolworths	42.4%
Computershare	53.5%
Tabcorp Holdings	67.5%

Interest cover

Most companies borrow to finance their operations, and they are obliged to repay the money at regular intervals, even if business turns sluggish. The interest cover ratio looks at the relationship between interest payments and profits in order to see if the company has a healthy margin of profit to protect it against a business downturn or against a sharp rise in interest rates.

The danger of a low ratio is that, if the economy turns bad and profits shrink, the company will effectively have to pay all its earnings as interest payments, leaving nothing for the shareholders. If this situation persists, the company's existence may be in doubt.

The interest cover ratio is expressed in times, and is also known as the 'times interest earned' ratio. It shows the number of times that interest charges could have been paid by pre-tax profit. A rough rule of thumb says that companies should be able to cover their interest payments at least three times. In other words, investigate thoroughly any company with a ratio of less than three. The formula is:

$$\text{Interest cover} = \text{EBIT} \div \text{net interest payments}$$

Net interest payments are the company's interest payments minus its interest receipts.

Table 8.4 shows examples of interest cover for the eight selected Australian companies.

Table 8.4: interest cover for the selected Australian companies, June 2011

Company	Times
BHP Billiton	56.7
Computershare	14.3
Woolworths	12.5
Harvey Norman Holdings	11.6
Tabcorp Holdings	6.7
Australian Securities Exchange (ASX)	—
Monadelphous Group	—
Wotif.com Holdings	—

For three of the companies it was not possible to calculate a ratio, because their high cash holdings meant their interest receipts were higher than their interest payments, giving them a negative interest cover figure.

Stock market ratios

A company might have high profits, low debt and strong growth prospects, suggesting it's a good investment, but its share price has been soaring. Do you still buy? The following ratios can be used to determine whether a share is cheap or expensive:

- earnings per share (EPS)
- price/earnings (P/E) ratio
- price-earnings-to-growth (PEG) ratio

- dividend yield
- net tangible assets (NTA) per share ratio.

Earnings per share

The earnings per share (EPS) is needed to calculate the important price/earnings ratio. Given its significance as a primary ratio, the figure is included in company annual reports, so you will seldom need to calculate it yourself. The formula is:

Earnings per share = after-tax profits ÷ number of shares

The number of shares needs to be a weighted average of those on issue during the year and this number is always included in company annual reports.

You should not try to compare the EPS figures for different companies, as this has no meaning. However, the year-on-year trend in EPS for a single company is of interest: it is often one of the first ratios checked by institutional investors and other professionals when they start checking out a stock.

Price to earnings ratio

Price to earnings (P/E) is a fundamental ratio, used and understood by most investors and even cited in media reports on the stock market. It is a very easy calculation. The formula is:

P/E ratio = latest share price ÷ EPS

Make sure you use the same price units in calculating the P/E ratio. The EPS figure will probably be in cents, not dollars, so make sure the share price is too. The ratio changes as the share price changes, which can be every minute. Some newspapers publish the ratio every day, and it is also available on some company websites, so you won't usually have to work it out yourself.

This ratio expresses the amount of money investors are ready to pay for each cent or dollar of a company's profits. It allows you to compare the share prices of different companies with widely different profits. A high P/E ratio suggests the market has a high regard for the company; a low one might mean the market is disdainful of the stock. In fact, the P/E ratio may sometimes work best in telling you how other investors regard the company's prospects.

Unfortunately, the P/E ratio is best employed for future profits, rather than for those that have already been announced. The reason is that the ratio is used to judge whether a stock is cheap or expensive, and stock market investors look to a company's future outlook, rather than its past performance, when setting prices.

This poses a problem for the home investor, who will not usually have the experience or the resources to calculate a future EPS, on which the P/E ratio is based. Analysts employed by stockbroking houses make these calculations, and you will probably be dependent on them.

As a very general rule, the P/E ratio will move according to profit expectations regarding a company and the risk involved with these earnings, though market sentiment is important too. For example, investors are usually more willing to put their money into stocks when interest rates are low than when they are high and even a bank savings account might offer a good return. And share prices—and hence P/E ratios—incorporate investor perceptions of not only the particular company but also such concerns as national and international economies, and global politics.

Whole books get written about how to find low-P/E-ratio stocks, and there are so many rules of thumb about the 'correct' P/E ratio that it is probably useless to worry about them.

One example is the complicated formula developed by Benjamin Graham, known as the dean of American security analysis. He linked long-term bond yields to the forecast growth rate for a company over seven to 10 years to determine the P/E ratio at which a share should be trading. However, the formula was devised when corporate growth was far more predictable than it is now. How many investors in Australia are prepared to hazard a guess on likely profit growth rates for a company for the next two or three years, let alone seven or 10?

Nevertheless, it is true that when a company's P/E ratio gets out of step with its historical P/E ratio—either much higher or much lower—it might eventually drift back into line, all else being equal. Even so, it may still enjoy a substantial and sustained period of under- or over-performance in the meantime, perhaps depending on what the market as a whole is doing.

In fact, there are many reasons why a particular stock might have a comparatively low or high P/E ratio, and sometimes these reasons are far from clear. You could get guidance somewhere in a company's annual report, but in such cases you might need to consult a good stockbroker.

Price-earnings-to-growth ratio

The internet has had a huge impact on the sharemarket, changing the way many investors do their business. That includes the advent of sites that allow you to carry out quite detailed analyses of specific stocks.

Surprisingly, the internet has even created a vogue for a new ratio—price earnings to growth (PEG).

One of the most popular American investment websites is Motley Fool <www.fool.com>. It contains a huge amount of investor information, including lessons in company analysis. The editors of Motley Fool claim to have invented the PEG ratio, which they call the Fool Ratio.

The PEG ratio is based on the proposition that a stock's P/E ratio should be roughly equivalent to its expected annual profit growth rate. That is, a company that is likely to have annual profit growth of 15 per cent for the next few years should be on a P/E of 15. If the expected annual growth rate is 25 per cent the P/E should be 25, and so on. The formula is:

$$\text{PEG ratio} = \text{P/E ratio} \div \text{expected annual EPS growth rate}$$

If the PEG ratio is higher than 1, the stock is expensive. If it is less than 1, then it is cheap.

The main problem, of course, is how to work out the expected annual EPS growth rate. This is what the highly paid analysts at stockbroking houses do all the time, and they base their forecasts on interviews with senior company executives, on the reports of their own in-house economists and on a raft of other data. The home analyst rarely has the luxury of such resources, and will probably have to rely on the forecasts contained in broking reports and investor newsletters, and there can sometimes be variations in these forecasts.

How far ahead should you try to forecast growth? Motley Fool looks ahead two years. Some other experts advocate five years, but not many analysts in Australia are prepared to make a five-year forecast for a company's profits.

How do you use the PEG ratio? Motley Fool suggests that if a stock has a ratio below 0.5 (that is, the expected annual profit growth rate is more than double the P/E ratio) then that stock is a Buy. If the PEG ratio is between 0.5 and 1.0, you should buy or hold. Between 1.0 and 1.3, you should think about selling. Between 1.3 and 1.7, you should think about short-selling the stock (that is, profiting from a falling stock price). And once the ratio is over 1.7 you should almost certainly short-sell the stock.

Motley Fool itself says the ratio works best with smaller stocks, on the basis that the bigger the company is, the less likely it is to be valued just from earnings.

In any case, dividends play a central role in the strategies of many Australian investors, and probably more so than in the United States. Some experts believe that a company's dividend yield is one of the best gauges of whether a stock is cheap or expensive.

Dividend yield

The dividend yield is the return on each individual share: the dividend expressed as a percentage of the latest share price.

It is a useful ratio, especially for those who are investing for the dividend, rather than for capital appreciation, as it allows you to compare the returns of various shares with each other, as well as with alternatives, such as a long-term bank deposit.

However, it is necessary to take tax implications into account when making comparisons. A low dividend may offer tax advantages, thanks to franking credits (discussed later in this section), and so be worth more to some investors than a higher bank account return. (When you are making investment decisions try, if possible, to use next year's likely dividend. Companies often provide forward guidance on profits and dividends through the financial media and on their websites.)

The dividend yield changes with moves in the share price, and the latest figures are published daily in many newspapers and are available on some websites. There is little need to work the yield out yourself, although it is extremely easy. The formula is:

Dividend yield = (dividend ÷ latest share price) × 100

Although most investors might prefer a stock with a high dividend yield to a stock with a low yield, that's not necessarily the best guide. Some companies, especially new and growing ones, prefer to pay a minimal dividend—or no dividend at all—so they can plough the bulk of profits back into the company to fuel further growth. Investors in such companies should eventually, in theory, be rewarded for the small dividend payout by the sharp capital appreciation of their shares.

There is a body of investment opinion in the United States which states that if you have a choice of buying a stock with a dividend yield of, say, 2 per cent and one with a yield of 7 per cent, and you know absolutely nothing else about either company, then you should choose the former. The reason is that a low dividend yield could indicate a growth company, and a high yield a fairly stagnant—albeit profitable—corporation. Of course, this reasoning assumes that an investor is seeking growth over income, which is not always the case.

However, the Australian system of franking credits makes the position here even more complicated. Dividend imputation, or franking, is a system that allows companies to pass tax credits on to shareholders. If a company has already paid taxes in Australia on its profits, then an investor receiving a dividend from that company can use that already-paid tax to offset his or her own income tax. Dividend imputation is not necessarily a complicated subject, but if you wish to buy shares to take advantage of franking credits, you would be advised to talk to a stockbroker, financial adviser or accountant to ensure that your financial strategy is sound.

Note that a steadily rising dividend—not the dividend yield, but the actual dividend—suggests that the company's management is reasonably confident about the future. Just as a dividend cut sends a bad signal to investors, an increased dividend is a good sign.

Net tangible assets per share ratio

The net tangible assets (NTA) per share ratio tells you what the company's tangible assets are theoretically worth, per share, after it has paid off all its liabilities. Intangibles—such as the goodwill on an acquisition or the value of a newspaper masthead—are excluded because of problems in valuing them, and also because they may have limited value if they were separated from the company and sold. (Of course, obvious tangible assets, such as plant, property and stock, are always included.) The formula is:

$$\text{NTA per share ratio} = (\text{shareholders' equity} - \text{intangibles}) \div \text{number of shares}$$

Shareholders' equity is used because it equals assets minus liabilities.

This ratio is one way of measuring whether a company's shares are cheap or expensive. In theory, if the NTA per share value is more than the share price, then the company is undervalued—a corporate raider could buy up all the shares, pay off the debt and other liabilities, and then sell the remaining assets for a profit.

But there are many problems with this theory. The assets will not necessarily fetch their book value if they are placed on the market. In any case, many sophisticated investors keep a check on a company's

NTA figure, although if a company's share price is sold down there is often a good reason. Investors normally buy shares in a company for its future profit stream, not its assets. It is profits that are at the heart of share valuation, not assets. This explains why many companies' share prices are higher—sometimes considerably higher—than their NTA per share figure.

Even when you do buy a company for its assets, such as for a new gold mine or an extensive underused inner-city property, these assets must eventually produce profits if they are to benefit the company and its shareholders.

Also, many companies have assets and liabilities that are not recorded on the balance sheet. These include good or bad management, high or low market share, superior or obsolete production techniques, and a good or bad reputation for quality. It is said that, in many companies, especially in the service sector, the most valuable assets go home each evening.

And though intangible assets are excluded because of difficulties in valuing them, the fact is that some companies own very extensive portfolios of valuable intangible assets.

Some companies also have assets that are worth more than their book values. For example, in many cases properties are valued only about every three years, and it is possible, through inflation or for other reasons, such as rezoning, for a particular piece of land to sharply appreciate in value between valuations.

It is difficult for an outsider to do much about this unless they know the exact size and location of a company's properties, and have some knowledge of valuation. Some securities analysts and corporate raiders devote much time to discovering the true worth of a company's assets.

As with the EPS ratio, there is no point in comparing different companies' NTA per share ratios. But it is possible to make a comparison of price to NTA per share ratio, which is simply a company's share price divided by its NTA per share (normally denoted as P/A ratio). A figure of 1 means the company is valued in line with its net tangible assets. Below this and, in theory, it is a bargain stock, priced below its true value.

It is also possible to calculate a price- to book-value ratio, by adding back intangibles to the formula. Many analysts prefer this ratio, on the grounds that many intangibles do have a value, and that investors should recognise this.

Chapter 9

Searching for income shares

So as you can see from Martin's discussion of fundamental analysis in chapter 8, a plethora of ratios and fundamental factors can be considered when you are analysing publicly listed companies. Furthermore, different analysts use different combinations of all these factors, generating a vast array of views and opinions. Whether this is a good thing or not is another matter, given the sheer volume of opinions being proffered every day in the financial media.

I face the same problem as everyone else on this score, and to solve this dilemma I simply employ the tried and tested fundamental criteria used by Stock Doctor to filter its shortlist of preferred stocks, called Star Stocks. The selection criteria used by Stock Doctor are different for each industry group (which makes a lot of sense) and these criteria are proprietary information.

You can also use Martin Roth's annual publication, *Top Stocks*, which shortlists about 100 stocks each year that Martin considers to be the best blue chip shares from a fundamental perspective. What's more, Martin outlines his selection criteria at the start of the book in case readers are interested in knowing it. Anyway, you will find advertisements for both these products at the back of this book.

But now I'll get back to my own knitting, which is how to hunt down potential asset-class shares. The last criterion we were looking at before I handed over to Martin for chapter 8 was the question of quality and how to determine value for money. Now that we've added fundamental analysis to our toolbox we can set about the task of answering these questions.

Quality and value (continued)

This section covers two very important areas to assess in deciding which shares to buy: quality and value for money.

We'll start with setting a benchmark for quality, and, as I've indicated, my filter for this is Stock Doctor's Star Stocks criteria. A share that Stock Doctor considers to be a Star Stock will be deemed to be a quality stock by me.

But no matter how good the quality of a company, I always like to pay as little as possible for my income stocks. So in order to know that I'm getting value for money, I'm going to employ two key stock market ratios:

- The first is the price to earnings (P/E) ratio, which is calculated by dividing the share price by the earnings per share.
- The other one is the price to net tangible assets per share (P/A) ratio. It is calculated by dividing the share price by the NTA per share.

We must ensure that the P/E and P/A ratios indicate value for money by being within acceptable benchmarks.

A low P/A ratio indicates that the asset backing of a company is proportionally high in comparison with its share price, whereas the opposite is true for a high P/A ratio. Interestingly, it is possible to find companies with P/A ratios of less than 1, which means that a $1 share represents more than $1 of value in net tangible assets. This situation occurs when the future prospects of a company are poor and the marketplace is more focused on earnings rather than asset backing.

To ensure that we don't buy shares in companies like this, we need to look for companies with both a low P/A ratio, indicating substantial asset backing, *and* a low P/E ratio, indicating good earnings. The minimum benchmarks I've used for the past two decades, which have worked very well, are a P/E ratio of 15 or less and a P/A ratio of 5 or less.

These minimum levels for earnings and asset backing will generally ensure that we are getting value for money when we shop for potential asset-class shares. And that's exactly what we're about to do next.

Market searches

With the aid of the Stock Doctor program, we can now run an automated search across the entire Australian stock market for possible candidates for investment.

We'll start by making a list of the mechanical benchmarks that we have developed for scanning the market for potential asset-class shares. This list excludes any discretionary guidelines, such as life expectancy, and so you'll see that I keep referring to 'potential' asset-class shares, because we have to take into account these other considerations as well.

Here are the mechanical criteria that we can input into Stock Doctor's stock filter function to scan the market in the search for suitable shares:

- market capitalisation—at least $100 million
- dividend yield—greater than the RBA target cash rate
- quality—companies that are currently Stock Doctor Star Stocks
- value—a P/E ratio equal to or less than 15 and a P/A ratio equal to or less than 5.

Using these benchmarks we can create a shortlist of potential asset-class shares, which is one of the searches we run every week in my ActVest newsletter (see the end of this book for more details). In fact, we've been running these scans for a very long time, and the rest of this chapter will look at some of the more interesting lists that these searches have returned over the years.

Before we do that, I want to show you a long-term chart of the All Ordinaries index, highlighting the major highs and lows in our market over the past decade. These are the moments in our recent history that we'll be examining more closely (see figure 9.1).

Figure 9.1: All Ordinaries index major highs and lows, 2000–12

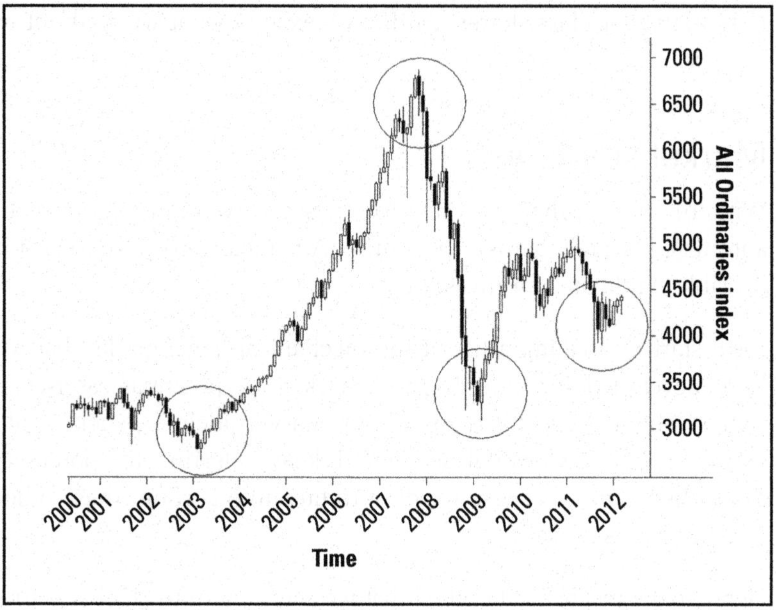

Source: MetaStock.

Search results from August 2011

I'm going to start with a look at a list of shares from the most recent market low, which occurred in August and September 2011. I'm then going to examine each of the potential asset-class shares on the list for their suitability as lifetime assets. When we ran a market scan earlier, using the criteria specified back in August 2011, we got the list of shares shown in table 9.1.

Table 9.1: asset-class shares from August 2011
(RBA cash rate = 4.75 per cent)

Company	Code	P/A ratio	P/E ratio	Dividend yield
ANZ Banking Group	ANZ	1.80	9.00	7.23%
Breville Group	BRG	4.44	11.55	4.83%
Cedar Woods Properties	CWP	1.62	6.44	5.51%
Gazal Corporation	GZL	2.57	10.33	6.91%
Minara Resources	MRE	0.90	12.60	7.94%
Thorn Group	TGA	4.06	10.11	4.80%

The official RBA target cash rate was 4.75 per cent at the time, and we always specify the current rate with the search results. As you can see, there were six candidates on our list and we always include the relevant ratios and their dividend yields, excluding any tax credits. So now I'll give you a quick opinion on each of these companies as possible income stocks:

- *ANZ.* I really liked this one at the time and in fact I bought it. ANZ and all the other leading banks were yielding just over 10 per cent per year when their franking (tax) credits were taken in account. I believe that our four leading banks will be around for my lifetime and whilst there have been many concerns expressed about their future prospects, I don't share these concerns. Our leading banks have proven time and time again that they know how to exploit both good times and bad, and they display a resilience akin to cockroaches in a nuclear holocaust.

- *BRG.* I liked this one and I bought it as well. BRG is a toilet paper–type company, as it produces toasters and kettles and other everyday products that we all use. I believe, therefore, that there is every possibility that it will be around for my lifetime. A more detailed examination of its management and historical performance didn't reveal any obvious issues. If anything, the biggest danger is that it's a takeover target for another company — an occupational hazard with good asset-class shares.

- *CWP.* Cedar Woods Properties is a real estate management and development company with interests in Western Australia and Victoria. I don't like it as a lifetime asset-class share, for two key reasons: the first one is that the collapse of Centro Property Group in 2008 highlighted the lack of transparency in the financials of property managers, and the use of dubious practices in asset valuation. The second reason is that I believe the fortunes of this company are closely linked to the resources boom in Perth and so it is a cyclical business (in which profitability rises and falls in sympathy with the economic cycle) and not really a lifetime asset.

- *GZL*. Gazal Corporation specialises in developing and building national and international brands in the apparel and fashion accessories industry. Therefore, I don't like it. Get next season's fashions wrong and the balance sheet turns into a sea of red. This is not the stuff that lifetime income-producing assets are made of.

- *MRE*. Minara Resources is principally a nickel-mining company. Again, resource companies are cyclical by nature and very much subject to the foibles of technological change, and so they are generally unsuited to being held as lifetime income-producing assets. Mind you, they can and often do make wonderful growth stocks.

- *TGA*. Thorn Group is the parent company of Radio Rentals, which is a household name that has been around for many years. It uses a seriously boring but proven business model of renting TVs and other household electrical goods, which is a very defensive business (in other words, it is largely immune from economic cycles as there is a fairly constant demand for its product) — so defensive in fact, that about 40 per cent of its client base is on some form of social welfare. So I think it's an ideal income share and I bought it.

You can see from my brief analysis here that we are seeking fairly boring companies that are involved in boring industries where things rarely, if ever, change much. This is for good reason and exactly in keeping with Warren Buffett's thinking when he bought stock in Gillette and Coca-Cola. If we want companies that will be around for our lifetime then we need to target ones that are very stable and operating in low-tech and very stable industry sectors.

Search results from March 2003

If you go back to the chart of the All Ordinaries in figure 9.1, you will note that the low in August and September 2011 wasn't really the lowest of lows, so now I want to go back to the far more significant low that occurred in March 2003 and show you the number of asset-class shares on the list at that time (see table 9.2).

Table 9.2: asset-class shares from March 2003 (RBA cash rate = 4.75 per cent)

Company	Code	P/A ratio	P/E ratio	Dividend yield
Alesco Corp	ALS	3.01	11.59	7.26%
AlintaGas	ALN	2.86	11.55	5.95%
AV Jennings Homes	AVJ	1.15	6.08	10.89%
Bristile	BRS	2.12	11.64	5.41%
Crane Group	CRG	1.60	10.19	7.13%
FKP Limited	FKP	1.10	7.98	7.09%
Freedom Group	FFL	4.44	10.50	6.15%
G.U.D. Holdings	GUD	3.30	10.52	5.03%
Gazal Corporation	GZL	3.00	12.99	6.08%
GES International	GEE	1.16	9.18	5.83%
Globe International	GLB	1.82	2.54	21.71%
Leighton Holdings	LEI	3.63	13.32	5.03%
Orica	ORI	2.30	11.20	5.12%
Pacifica Group	PBB	1.92	11.87	5.52%
Programmed Maintenance	PRG	1.67	8.01	4.85%
Schaffer Corporation	SFC	3.78	10.10	6.79%
Simsmetal	SMS	2.67	12.26	5.10%

Again, the RBA's target cash rate at the time was 4.75 per cent and as you can see there was a wide range of choice, with 17 stocks coming up on the list. When the market is depressed, as it was in March of 2003, there is plenty of value to be found and loads of income stocks to choose from. If you were a growth investor, however, it would have been a very depressing period.

Search results from November 2007

Now compare the number of shares in March 2003 with the search results from November 2007, when the broader market was at an all-time high (see table 9.3).

Table 9.3: asset-class shares from November 2007
(RBA cash rate = 6.75 per cent)

Company name	Code	P/A Ratio	P/E Ratio	Dividend yield
Colonial First Private Capital	CFI	0.92	7.05	11.54%
City Pacific	CIY	2.79	7.55	12.16%
Minara Resources	MRE	3.85	6.03	11.20%
WAM Capital	WAM	0.94	3.97	8.99%
Zinifex	ZFX	3.19	5.64	9.06%

This meagre list offers only five companies, and two of those are resource stocks and are therefore immediately eliminated—in my view, anyway. Other stocks that qualify for immediate elimination are the listed fund managers, such as CFI and WAM, as they themselves are invested in the stock market and are by their very nature growth stocks and not income stocks—their fortunes will go up and down with the rise and fall of the stock market. What's more, the likelihood of these entities being around for my lifetime is very low, given that listed funds usually have a fixed life expectancy anyway. In fact, Colonial First Private Capital delisted in December of 2007. Listed funds aren't really lifetime propositions, one of the essential criteria for asset-class shares.

Search results from March 2009

So you can see that there were very slim pickings for asset-class shares at the peak of 2007. But, as you will no doubt recall if you were watching the stock market at the time, or if you look to the chart of the All Ords in figure 9.1 (see p. 134), it then plummeted from its peak in November 2007 to the extreme low of March 2009.

When markets rise there are more and more growth stocks to choose from, but when they fall, there are more and more income stocks to choose from. And to prove the point we'll now take a look at the search results from the major market low of March 2009 (see table 9.4).

Table 9.4: asset-class shares from March 2009 (RBA cash rate = 3.25 per cent)

Company name	Code	P/A ratio	P/E ratio	Dividend yield
Ansell	ANN	3.63	9.34	3.43%
ARB Corporation	ARP	2.34	8.40	5.87%
Austbrokers Holdings	AUB	4.79	11.88	5.14%
Centennial Coal Company	CEY	1.13	6.94	13.95%
Campbell Brothers	CPB	3.92	5.22	11.52%
Felix Resources	FLX	3.12	5.13	7.20%
Fleetwood Corporation	FWD	2.07	5.79	5.97%
IMF (Australia)	IMF	2.12	3.70	10.00%
Leighton Holdings	LEI	2.70	8.28	7.13%
Mineral Resources	MIN	2.48	5.91	8.48%
OM Holdings	OMH	2.20	4.86	5.68%
SMS Management & Technology	SMX	3.10	4.96	12.89%
Servcorp	SRV	1.31	4.92	7.81%
Steamships Trading Company	SST	2.10	7.86	9.04%

As you can see, March 2009 was a very different situation from November 2007, and while this list included quite a few resource stocks and listed funds, there were some real gems scattered about as well. You'll also note that the RBA cash rate will inevitably fall in sympathy with a weakening economy, which also helps the list increase, as it is one of our benchmarks.

There were 14 shares on the list in March 2009, and some pretty impressive yields to boot. And while I don't want to drill down into them too far, the standouts for me that I highlighted at the time were Campbell Brothers, ARB Corporation and Fleetwood Corporation.

All three of these are defensive stocks: Campbell Brothers sells basic food items; ARB sells automotive 4×4 accessories; and Fleetwood sells caravans and low-cost portable accommodation solutions. When times are tough, we still have to eat, and we tend to take cheap holidays like road trips and engage in affordable leisure activities like 4×4 driving and camping.

I'm giving you my opinion on these shares, but that's not to say that some readers and other experts won't have different opinions. There are many factors that one can take into account when assessing the suitability of income stocks and it is a very discretionary area of investment. But what I am trying to communicate in this discussion is the common considerations that all income investors should include in their investment framework.

A time to buy

So there's a time to buy income stocks and there's a time to focus on other things, like growth stocks. When the stock market is at or near a major high and share prices are up, then value is hard to find and there are very few opportunities. But when the market is defining a major low and the asset-class shares list swells, as it did in March 2003 and March 2009, then it's definitely time to be hunting for income stocks.

You'll also notice that when markets are severely depressed Warren Buffett is running around with his chequebook, acquiring large chunks of companies and getting himself in the financial news. Buffett is looking for attractive income streams from well-established businesses: one example is when he bought $3 billion worth of preferred stock in General Electric with a guaranteed 10 per cent annual distribution. He negotiated this deal when the US markets were in the grips of the global financial crisis (GFC) in mid 2008 (see figure 9.2).

Figure 9.2: General Electric — share price and volume of sales in 2008

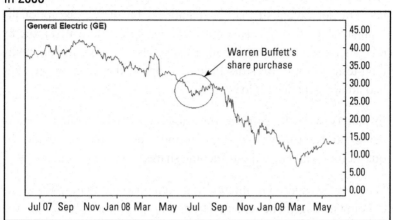

Other notable acquisitions by Warren Buffett during the GFC were $5 billion worth of preferred stock in Bank of America, and a $5 billion investment in Goldman Sachs. Interestingly, the Goldman Sachs deal also included a 10 per cent yield, and it would appear that Buffett is quite happy with this income benchmark. So I guess he would have been quite happy buying shares in ANZ in August 2011, when it had a grossed up yield of just over 10 per cent.

But there are two key points to note here: there's a time to buy and when that time comes there are only a few really outstanding opportunities. Income stocks don't grow on trees in the way growth stocks sometimes do. In a raging bull market there can be so many growth stocks to choose from that you simply won't know where to put your money. But not so with income stocks.

So a choosy income investor should expect to acquire only a handful of new asset-class shares every decade or so, much in keeping with Warren Buffett's buying pattern. Furthermore, when the time comes to pounce we must have the confidence to act, because when markets are depressed and falling, all the talk and commentary will be extremely negative.

In fact, when I bought ANZ in August 2011, I was very surprised to hear even some seasoned investors suggesting our banks could fail. I'm not saying this couldn't happen, but it was exceptionally unlikely given their fundamentals and, I suspect, motivated more by the general fear at the time than anything else. For that reason, many long-term income investors didn't swoop on the banks when they had an ideal chance to do so.

In part IV we will return to the subject of market timing in more detail, but right now we're going to move on to chapter 10 and the question of when to sell our income shares.

While it is never our intention to sell income shares, there are ongoing management considerations, and given the right (or should I say wrong) circumstances, we may have to part company with some of our income-producing assets.

Chapter 10

Managing income shares

Now it's time to get down to the nitty-gritty of how to manage our asset-class shares. As part of this explanation I will be reiterating some of the key concepts made in the previous chapters. I'll start with the point that we are searching for attractive income streams rather than capital gains. This is the flip side of what we do as traders or investors seeking capital growth, and so when the market is falling and prices are dropping, dividend yields are rising, and it's a good time to buy asset-class shares.

As income investors our perspective is that we're buying the rising income stream and not the falling share price. This is the quintessential difference between growth and income investing and it is imperative that we are forever mindful of this fact, as it means that not only are our investment objectives virtually 180 degrees opposed, but so are the management requirements.

Capital allocation: growth versus income shares

We'll start with what is probably the most obvious management issue of all, and one of the few questions that I can't give a definitive answer to.

How much of my total capital should I allocate to my income portfolio and how much do I allocate to growth stocks? I can't provide a general answer to this question, as we are all in very different situations.

Each of us must decide for ourselves how much of our total capital we want to allocate to asset-class shares versus trading shares. Once we've made up our minds, then we need to split our money into two separate pools and treat them as mutually exclusive. When pondering this question you could consider the following points:

- Income shares require very little management and generally need to be reviewed only once a year, while growth shares are normally managed on a weekly basis. So while growth shares can provide a higher return, they definitely require more effort.

- Typically, the younger you are, the more inclined you will be to actively manage your shares. Hence growth shares will be more attractive to you at this time, but as you get on in life you may want to gradually migrate your capital across to your income portfolio. Also, nicely matured income stocks, like CBA shares bought in the original float back in 1991, represent less risk than growth shares bought more recently.

- As the intention is to hold income shares indefinitely, you must assume that you won't have ready access to the capital you allocate to them (fixed assets), while shares that you trade can be sold quickly and turned to cash (liquid assets).

Whatever mix you choose can change over time, and so I wouldn't dwell on it too much. Also, the amount of money you have to play with will have some bearing as well, because if you only have a very small amount of money then it may be a case of having either an income or a growth portfolio, as opposed to having both.

Risk management

While capital allocation is open to individual interpretation, the question of risk management isn't, and risk management of income shares differs considerably from that of growth shares. The key difference is that income, or asset-class, shares, given their buy and hold nature, can't employ a stop loss.

And unfortunately there is always the chance that a stock that can look very attractive on paper can turn out to be a complete dud. Just ask anyone who bought insurance company HIH back in the 1990s.

Because we can't apply a stop loss to our income shares, the only protection we have is diversification. I never allocate more than 10 per cent of my total capital to one individual position, and when I conduct the annual review of my income portfolio, I sell down any position that has reached or exceeded 15 per cent of total capital to take the allocation back to 10 per cent of total capital.

This practice may also vary according to the amount of capital you are investing and your level of risk aversion. If you have a very large amount of capital or a high aversion to risk, or both, then you may want to limit the initial purchase to 5 per cent of total capital and trim it back if it ever gets to 10 per cent of total capital. However, this will result in a portfolio of approximately 20 individual positions and I would never want to diversify beyond this level.

The Australian stock market isn't that big, and there aren't that many opportunities to be had, so finding 20 really attractive income shares will prove hard enough, and going beyond this number will inevitably involve some degree of compromise. Introducing compromise into the selection process means an increase in risk. So there is an optimal level of diversification and I believe it lies somewhere between 10 and 20 positions.

We also need to be mindful of our sector exposure, which I recommend be limited to 25 per cent of total capital in any one sector at the time of purchase. Our level of exposure to each sector will vary over time, as the prices of our shares move up and down, so this also requires an ongoing management approach, such as position sizing, and so I will return to this issue further on.

Reviewing your income shares

Now to the routine part of income portfolio management, which includes when and how to review your income shares and what you should be looking for. There are several things you need to consider, but uppermost in your mind should be whether each of your income-producing assets is producing an adequate amount of income. And will they keep doing so?

Yearly review

But there are other considerations as well, the most obvious being the question of when we should review our income portfolio. Happily, the answer here is just as obvious: I recommend that you review your income portfolio once a year. But I'm going to digress slightly here and also recommend that, while we're at it, we also review our capital or asset allocation.

Capital or asset allocation

We need to check and ensure that we are not too heavily weighted in any particular asset class. This is an exercise that all investors should perform on an annual basis and one that I believe becomes far more critical if we are in or approaching retirement.

This is because an imbalance in our asset allocation can expose us to the totally unnecessary risk of a catastrophic event occurring within a single asset class, such as a stock market crash. Let's assume you have your money spread across the asset classes shown in figure 10.1.

Figure 10.1: main asset classes

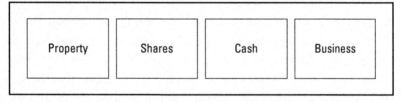

| Property | Shares | Cash | Business |

Here's a suggested set of sensible guidelines for the average baby boomer—the generation that has just retired or will retire soon:

- Have enough cash to live on for at least two years in case of a general downturn.
- Don't allow shares to exceed property assets (very pertinent during a market boom).

- Retain your business interests, if possible, in case of a general downturn.

- Make sure your assets are legally protected, especially if you are in business.

- Establish or manage financial structures to minimise tax and reduce legal exposure.

This is exactly the sort of exercise you would expect to undertake each year under the guiding hand of your financial planner or personal wealth manager. This is a process that you should be actively involved in, and it should always include a review of your financial structures. Of course there is no reason why you can't do this exercise by yourself, but the key point here is to do it.

Yield remains attractive

Back to the topic at hand and, more specifically, the core issue of income yield. This is central to the review of our income portfolio: are our assets producing adequate income and are they likely to keep doing so? You must ensure that you make this assessment based on your initial purchase price, increased using the cost of living through a suitable benchmark, such as a realistic annual Consumer Price Index (CPI) figure, and not the current share price and dividend yield.

This is such an important part of the annual review process, that it is probably best if I demonstrate how this is done with a working example.

Let's take the fairly straightforward case of CBA shares, which we'll assume you purchased around financial year 1991–92 at the bargain basement price of just $6.50. The question now is: what is your $6.50 worth today?

Just over 20 years on, your original $6.50 is now worth a lot more, largely due to the impact of inflation. In other words, $6.50 back in 1991–92 had a lot more purchasing power than it has today. However, we can calculate the equivalent value of $6.50 from 1991–92 by indexing it using a hypothetical (but indicative) annual CPI of 4 per cent.

This is done by simply multiplying $6.50 by a factor of 1.04 for every intervening financial year:

1991: $6.50

1992: $6.50 × 1.04 = $6.76

1993: $6.76 × 1.04 = $7.03

1994: $7.03 × 1.04 = $7.31

and so on, to

2012: $14.24 × 1.04 = $14.81

There you have it: $6.50 in 1991 is roughly equivalent in purchasing power to $14.81 today. Now we can compare CBA's current dividend payment to the current value of your original purchase price of $6.50, where CBA's annual dividend in 2012 is $3.25:

$3.25 ÷ $14.81 = 22% annual return, based on your original investment of $6.50

And after allowing for the 100 per cent franking credit:
22% ÷ 0.7 = 31% per year

Based on these numbers, I would say that CBA shares purchased in 1991–92 are now a very nicely matured income-producing asset.

Here are some other key points you will also want to consider when assessing a share's income:

- Is there an investment you can move my money into that has a better yield?
- Is the annual return on your investment increasing or decreasing each year?
- Were there any abnormals in the annual distribution to shareholders? (For instance, did the company sell off any major assets, creating one-off profit?)
- Is the value of the share dropping over time and therefore offsetting the income?

If these questions don't raise any concerns and the yield is attractive, then I would suggest that the share is generating an acceptable income stream, for now. And so I reiterate the need to perform this review at least once a year and not put your income shares in the bottom drawer and forget about them. With the business cycle getting shorter and shorter, I think those days are definitely over.

What not to do

What you don't want to do is fall for the trap of using the current dividend yield to assess your shares, because it is based on the current share price, which is not actually relevant to this assessment. Take the example of AV Jennings (AVJ), which was a very attractive income share back in 2002. Figure 10.2 is Stock Doctor's summary on AV Jennings, showing its key parameters from late 2002 to 2005.

Figure 10.2: Stock Doctor's summary of AV Jennings, September 2002 to September 2005

Company Summary for AVJennings Limited (AVJ)							
	Sep 02 Interim	Mar 03 Annual	Sep 03 Interim	Mar 04 Annual	Sep 04 Interim	Mar 05 Annual	Sep 05 Interim
Financial Health	Strong (.10)	Strong (.10)	Strong (.10)	Strong (.10)	Satis. (.11)	E. Warn (.49)	Marg (.70)
Annualised ROA	14.09%	18.25%	22.02%	17.96%	13.83%	6.17%	4.07%
Annualised ROE	30.21%	36.30%	45.35%	36.43%	29.43%	14.42%	9.88%
EPS	9.47 cps	26.37 cps	18.11 cps	31.81 cps	13.01 cps	12.75 cps	4.14 cps
EPS Growth 1 yr (%pa)	46.14% pa	93.44% pa	91.24% pa	20.63% pa	-28.16% pa	-59.90% pa	-68.20% pa
EPS Growth 2 yr (%pa)							
EPS Growth 3 yr (%pa)							
EPS Growth 4 yr (%pa)							
Revenue ($000)	$254,462	$529,249	$300,469	$552,136	$260,018	$439,108	$235,901
Adj. Profit Pre Tax ($000)	$29,057	$80,680	$55,816	$97,678	$39,928	$39,203	$12,677
Ex Dividend Date	29/11/2002	7/07/2003	1/12/2003	5/07/2004	30/11/2004	5/07/2005	5/01/2006
Franking	100%	100%	100%	100%	100%	100%	100%
DPS	3.00 cps	7.00 cps	3.50 cps	7.50 cps	3.50 cps	7.50 cps	2.50 cps
Dividend Yield	13.41%	9.71%	6.52%	4.80%	5.70%	8.33%	7.19%
PE	4.93	3.91	4.60	7.20	7.23	10.35	35.81
Industry Group Avg PE	12.31	12.33	11.83	11.94	11.87	12.51	15.17
PEG	0.11	0.04	0.05	0.35	N/A	N/A	N/A
Market Cap ($000)	$176,486	$221,683	$346,514	$492,868	$415,387	$284,099	$299,165
Fully Paid Ord. Shares (000)	215,226	215,226	215,226	215,226	215,226	215,226	215,226
Avg Dly Vol (22 days)	34,448	127,395	188,399	183,285	125,958	158,050	112,084
Avg Dly Traded	$30,786	$127,771	$296,907	$395,079	$236,536	$216,383	$154,840
Price	$0.82	$1.03	$1.61	$2.29	$1.93	$1.32	$1.39

Source: StockDoctor.

While it is an extreme example, the case of AV Jennings illustrates the point well. Looking at the first column for AV Jennings (Sep 02) you will see that, based on the share price at the time, the dividend yield was 13.41 per cent, with 100 per cent franking credits—very attractive in anyone's view. But one and a half years later (March 04), the dividend yield has dropped off dramatically to just 4.8 per cent, which would suggest that the actual dividend has more than halved.

But in fact the dividend payments to investors remained virtually unchanged, while the share price rose from about 80 cents to more than $2, making the yield drop dramatically. So the dividend yield can be very deceiving and you should always look at the dividend payment itself and, as stated earlier, compare it with your initial purchase price, indexed using the cost of living. Of course, with the doubling of AV Jennings share price its fundamentals became somewhat overstretched, but that is an issue that should be reviewed separately, which we'll now do.

Fundamentally sound

If we go back to the report on AV Jennings in figure 10.2, you can see that, as the share price rose dramatically, the fundamentals tapered off nearly as fast. I draw your attention to the row marked Financial Health which went from Strong in the Sep 02 column to Marginal by Sep 05, when the P/E ratio was 36 and the earnings per share growth (1 year) was well into negative territory.

Different industry groups require different benchmarks for what is acceptable and what isn't in terms of fundamentals. Given that it's not a case of one size fits all, I can't give a set of fixed parameters for when to sell income shares. But it's pretty clear in this instance that the alarms bells were ringing loudly for AV Jennings. This case also highlights the need to constantly monitor a company's financial ratios, as they can and will change.

Future prospects

Another related consideration is the assessment of a company's future prospects. Imagine owning a company that made buggy whips when cars were first introduced. While a buggy whip company could have had very good fundamentals and an attractive dividend yield, its days were certainly numbered, and I suspect its share price would have been gradually falling as a result.

What makes this assessment a bit tricky is its qualitative nature — there are no set benchmarks we can apply. However, for the sake of providing you with a working example: I'm a bit sceptical about Telstra and its ageing copper wire network. Furthermore, its long-held monopoly in the telecommunications sector is fast fading, as advancing technology is levelling the playing field.

In fact, I suspect Telstra is something of a corporate dinosaur and is in very real danger of ultimately being broken up. And I believe these poor future prospects are reflected in the long-term price behaviour of Telstra. In figure 10.3 you can see how Telstra is in a decade-long downtrend. Even a very attractive dividend yield in double digits isn't preventing this slide

Figure 10.3: Telstra, 2000–11

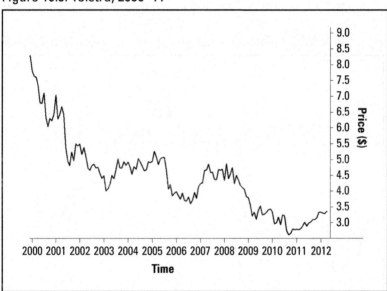

Source: MetaStock.

It's important to point out that, when buying an income share, we will tolerate a falling share price. In fact, for the first several years of ownership our overall return of capital growth plus dividend payments may well be negative. But a decade-long downtrend combined with poor future prospects is not to be ignored. So we must always be mindful of the long-term price trend and the future prospects of a company and its industry group.

Switching from an income share to a growth share

Returning to the example of AV Jennings, there is another option for those who purchased AVJ back in late 2002, and that was to switch it from being an income share to a growth share. The decision at the time would have been triggered by the sharp rise in its share price and the temptation to lock in this massive capital growth. Scan across the very last row at the bottom of the table in figure 10.2 (see p. 149), and you will see how its share price more than doubled over the period shown.

Making the switch would have meant applying a stop loss strategy and managing the share price as opposed to the income stream it provided through its dividend payments. Using a 20 per cent drawdown stop loss strategy, as explained back in part II, would have worked quite nicely. The chart in figure 10.4 shows how we would have exited AV Jennings when it breached the stop loss in mid 2004 at around $1.80.

Figure 10.4: AV Jennings—20 per cent drawdown stop loss, 2003–05

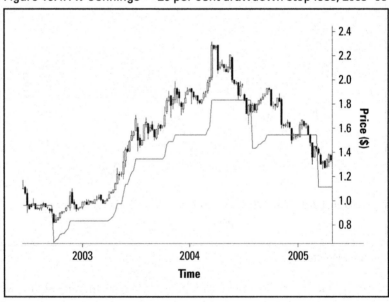

Source: MetaStock.

I personally would have been tempted to take this approach because a share price that doubles in the space of just one year will inevitably lead to overstretched fundamentals. This is because some key fundamental ratios (the stock market ratios explained in chapter 8) are linked to the share price and will indicate deteriorating value when subjected to a rising share price. Furthermore, you would have been forced to sell down this holding anyway to maintain a safe level of capital allocation. So it is possible to switch shares from income to growth shares and vice versa.

Portfolio rebalancing

This section follows on from our earlier discussion on risk management. As our only means of protection against catastrophic risk is diversification (given that we don't use stop losses to manage income stocks) then we must continually rebalance our portfolio. And, as previously stated, I personally like to ensure that each income stock remains somewhere between 10 and 15 per cent of the total portfolio value.

When I initially purchase income shares, I spend a maximum of 10 per cent of total capital, and when I do my annual review I will sell down any position that has reached or exceeded 15 per cent of total capital back to 10 per cent.

In our annual review, we also check our sector exposure, which I like to maintain at a maximum of no more than about 25 per cent of capital per sector. It is important to monitor and trim our sector exposure, as it is a common tripwire for longer term investors.

To emphasise this point I will relate the story of my doctor, who is probably one of the most conservative investors I know. All of his holdings are in the ASX top 25 stocks, and he would be lucky to execute a single transaction per year. In other words, he's the definition of a buy and hold investor. But as a result of this highly conservative approach, he was chronically overweight in bank stocks in late 2007, and paid the ultimate price when this sector was one of the worst hit in the GFC correction of 2008. Over the years he had purchased shares in our four leading banks, either during their stock placements or near their initial listings.

Given their massive share price growth over the years and because he had never bothered to rebalance his portfolio, he had more than half his capital in this one sector. Then the inevitable happened and 2008 gouged a very large hole in the value of his portfolio—a hole that would have been much smaller had he maintained less exposure to this one sector. Hedging during this time would also have helped considerably, and we'll look at this option more in part IV.

If you boil a frog slowly then he won't notice, and apparently the same goes for some investors. Of course, I can understand an income investor being attracted to the banking sector and maybe deliberately having 33 per cent of total capital exposed to it, but more than 50 per cent is clearly not prudent. My primary point here is that even income investors need to be mindful of their sector exposure.

Sensible benchmarks

The benchmarks suggested here are not set in stone, but are a sensible set of guidelines that are open to a degree of individual interpretation. Thus a seasoned income investor with a very large amount of capital may be inclined to use more conservative benchmarks, while a newer or younger investor with less risk aversion might lean the other way.

Without knowing your individual situation, I believe we have come as far as we possibly can with this discussion and its key aspects. However, there is one more topic that we need to look at, and that's market timing. There is a time to trade in growth shares and a time to accumulate income shares. So to ultimately succeed in the long term as investors, we must apply the right approach at the right time.

PART IV

Timing the market

Chapter 11

Introduction to market cycles

We are born. Our parents shelter, clothe, feed, protect and educate us. In doing so they spend money on certain services and products. Eventually we leave home, get married, buy a house and have children of our own, and the cycle of modern human life repeats itself. This pattern is inevitable and fairly predictable.

At each stage of our lives we belong to a different demographic group. Different demographic groups have different lifestyles, resulting in different needs and wants, which leads to quite different and distinct spending habits. Middle-aged people have families and generally work, while older people who are retired don't work and typically consume less.

These differing circumstances will largely dictate individuals' consumption habits and their contribution to the economy: that is, their productive output. Combining this information with population data provides powerful clues about the current and future direction of the broader economy. These financial patterns are inevitable and fairly predictable.

Some long-term economic analysts make a career out of studying these human/economic cycles and demographic groups. Governments, city planners and other regulators who have to think well ahead in terms of public demands, also study these cycles. This is an obvious example of cyclical analysis, with a very easily understood foundation.

We drive financial markets

The key point here is that we human beings drive economic cycles, and financial markets are simply a reflection of the economic systems on which they are based. Given the repetitive nature of life, cyclical analysis has a very strong and sound behavioural basis, and so ignorance of this science would not only be a bit silly, but financially foolhardy as well.

Since human beings drive markets, it is reasonable to assume that markets are a reflection of our behaviour. A couple of human traits, which are often reflected in financial markets, are that we resist change, so we tend to trend, and we like to think and project on a linear basis.

Figure 11.1 shows just over a decade of the All Ordinaries index from the early 1990s, and you can see how the market trended up the entire time. It also formed a near perfect trading channel with well-defined, straight-lined (linear) boundaries.

Figure 11.1: All Ordinaries index trading in a well-defined channel, 1991–2002

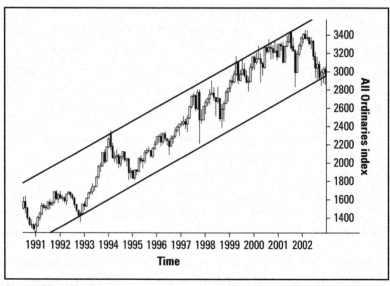

Source: MetaStock.

The amazing thing is that no regulating authority or single powerful investor is deliberately causing this almost perfect trading channel to occur: it is simply the result of mass human interaction. What's more, it isn't restricted to whole markets or just rising trends. Figure 11.2 shows another near-perfect example of a share over a decade-long period in a downtrend — Telstra.

Figure 11.2: Telstra trading in a well-defined falling channel, 2002–12

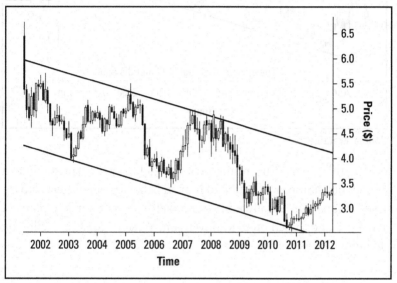

Source: MetaStock.

One of the oldest tools used by chartists is the humble trendline and, as you can see, for good reason. There are countless examples of this phenomenon occurring throughout the financial markets, and I will delve into a more detailed explanation of it in chapter 12.

Right now, I'm going to show you an equally compelling chart that defines a near perfect trading channel and also demonstrates the cyclical nature of financial markets. Figure 11.3 (overleaf), a chart of Western Areas mining, is following what appears to be an annual cycle.

Figure 11.3: Western Areas cycling up and down, 2004–06

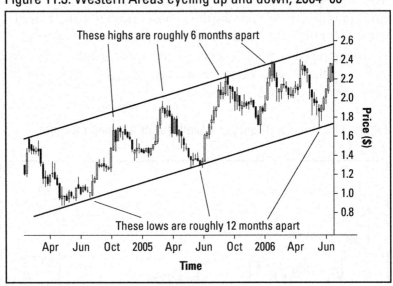

Source: MetaStock.

Again, this is not the result of some deliberate or premeditated action, but simply a reflection of human behaviour in market activity. Cyclical analysts usually employ market lows as their key point of reference and, based on this convention, Western Areas is cycling on an annual basis.

Time frame

Of course markets can cycle over many different time frames, ranging from several decades to just a few days. In the case of demographic cycles, we would typically be looking at periods like 20 to 30 years, which represents the start of each new generation; to the average human lifetime, which lies somewhere between 70 and 80 years.

Now to the shorter end of the spectrum. Figure 11.4 is an example of a daily price chart, for Ramsay Health, where price activity is cycling up and down over a period of just a few weeks. You'll note in this instance that the cycles are slightly irregular; this is not surprising, given that shorter cycles are predominantly less stable and therefore less regular than longer cycles are.

Figure 11.4: Ramsay Health cycling up and down

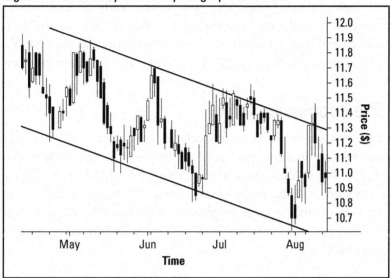

Source: MetaStock.

So there are short-, medium- and long-term cycles overlapping each other and causing all sorts of curious distortions and intermediate cycles. It all adds up to a bit of a mess, and the job of the cyclical analyst is to untangle it. One of the obvious ways of doing this is to find a particular perspective that you're comfortable with, and stick to it and its relevant time frame.

Different perspectives

Analysts can adopt a variety of perspectives. We've already covered the human life cycle and the use of demographics, but there are a variety of other commonly used approaches as well, including:

- macroeconomics
- fundamental or business analysis

- political or election cycles
- technical analysis.

For the purpose of having a well-grounded discussion, I'm ignoring the more eccentric methods, such as the study of lunar cycles, numerology and astrology, and so on. Just sticking to the more mainstream and robust approaches, let's investigate some examples of the application of these methods, starting with the economic clock.

The economic clock

The concept of the economic clock (see figure 11.5) has been around for decades and, until fairly recently, has been widely accepted doctrine when it comes to understanding how basic economic and business cycles work. There wouldn't be an economics student, past or present, who hasn't been exposed to the concept in Economics 101 and couldn't recreate it entirely from memory.

Figure 11.5: the economic clock

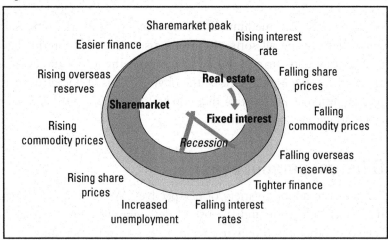

Moving around the clock in a clockwise direction indicates a set progression of key economic events and circumstances. Soon after the sharemarket peaks, interest rates will start to rise and then share prices will begin to fall, closely followed by falling commodity prices. Using this cycle of events as a guide, one can supposedly anticipate what's coming next and therefore what action is appropriate — buy shares, sell shares, buy property, pay down debt and so on.

It has also been conventional doctrine that the economic cycle lasts for about 10 years. But due to the introduction of economic stimulus by governments and key regulators in recent times, the economic clock has got a little out of whack.

Another influence that is partially responsible for the demise of the economic clock is Alan Greenspan, recent past chairman of the US Federal Reserve. Alan Greenspan championed the idea of taking a proactive approach to regulating an economy by anticipating future problems and tweaking monetary policy in advance. The jury is still out on whether this was or has been a successful innovation, but it is fairly certain that it's played havoc with the economic clock. Although I suspect the economic clock isn't about to disappear from the textbooks just yet.

Political influence

A slightly more fixed, and therefore predictable, cycle is the US political or election cycle. Every four years, in November, there is a presidential election, and it would be grossly naive to think that this would have no influence on financial markets.

But there is an interesting twist here, because if you simply look at the US S&P 500 index, with all the presidential elections highlighted over the past 40 years, there is no discernible pattern. However, if you only highlight the presidential elections where the incumbent is running for their second (and last) term in office (see figure 11.6, overleaf), then a subtle but consistent pattern does become apparent.

Figure 11.6: the S&P 500 index with second term US elections circled, 1972 to 2009

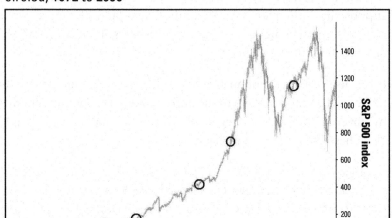

Source: MetaStock.

It's probably a bit hard to see in figure 11.6, but whenever a US president is seeking re-election, the S&P 500 is either rising or at the top of a market cycle. In other words, on six separate occasions over the past 40 years the US equity markets and the domestic economy in general have either been in pretty good shape or well and truly on the mend when a sitting president has gone to the polls.

Aggressive and direct manipulation of the US economy has only really been possible for about the past 40 years because before then the US dollar was pegged to the gold standard. Key regulators and government policy makers were largely unable to employ the types of stimulus measures that are readily available to them today. So for the past 40 years these same regulators and policy makers have had the motivation to window-dress the economy, and also the tools to do it. Call me a cynic.

We will revisit this phenomenon in chapter 13, where we will look at a very specific comparison between what happened 40 years ago and what's happening today in 2012. But now I want to go back in history even further to the late 1800s and the time of Charles Dow. This very famous forefather to modern technical analysis and co-founder of Dow Jones & Co. was in fact one of the very first cyclical analysts.

Early Dow theory

Charles Dow, while working as the editor of the *Wall Street Journal* in the latter half of the 1800s, made the observation that markets typically trend up in a series of three main waves. Hence they rise in three separate and distinct legs, which can easily be seen today on many long-term index charts. Here are some obvious examples, starting with the All Ordinaries index from the 1980s (see figure 11.7) and in the first decade of this century (see figure 11.8, overleaf), then the US S&P 500 from the mid 1990s (see figure 11.9, overleaf) and lastly China's Shanghai Composite index from 2006 to 2008 (see figure 11.10, on p. 167).

Figure 11.7: All Ordinaries index rising in three waves, 1980s

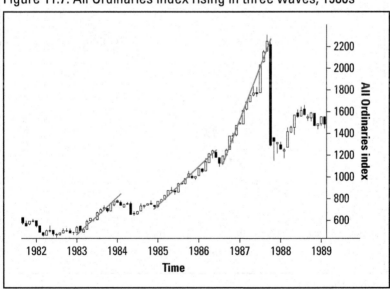

Source: MetaStock.

Figure 11.8: All Ordinaries index rising in three waves, 2003–08

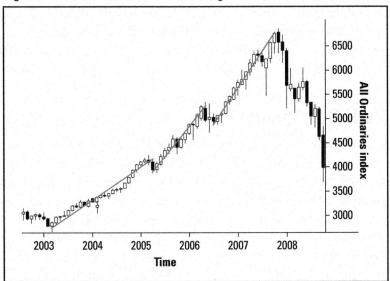

Source: MetaStock.

Figure 11.9: S&P 500 index rising in three waves, 1994–2000

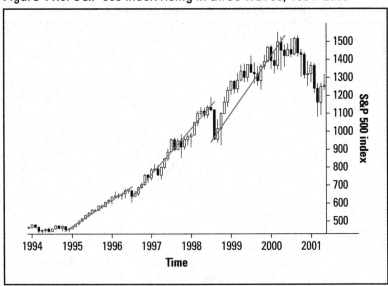

Source: MetaStock.

Figure 11.10: Shanghai Composite index rising in three waves, 2006–08

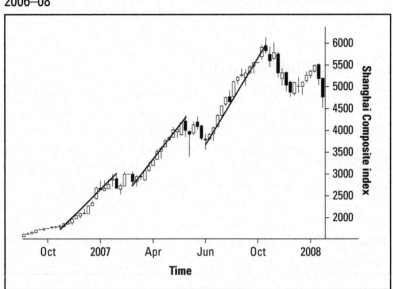

Source: MetaStock.

Describing price or market trends as a series of waves was one of the early parts of what is known today as Dow theory. Charles Dow went on to describe the psychology behind each wave and his overall theory also included the concept of sector rotation. However, sector rotation isn't relevant to this discussion and so we won't go into it.

Rather, the most obvious implication of Dow's earlier observation was that when you encounter the third leg up in a market rally, there is a very good chance the music is about to stop. Charles Dow never actually attempted to quantify his wave theory beyond the idea that there would typically be three main legs, a challenge that was to be taken up in the next century by Ralph Elliott, an accountant who made a systematic study of 75 years of stock market data—I will introduce Elliott wave principle (EWP) in chapter 12.

As you can see, cyclical analysis is a very broad field that has been around in one form or another for a very long time. It includes some very robust forms of analysis, side by side with some very eccentric ideas and approaches. So applying the same common sense philosophy I have towards fundamental and technical analysis, I recommend using cyclical analysis in its more robust form(s), coupled with a healthy appreciation of its limitations.

Cyclical analysis today

Although cyclical analysis is a long-established science, it is far from commonplace. I used a form of cyclical analysis to get out of the market in late 2007 and stay out until July 2009, completely avoiding the correction of 2008 (see figure 11.11). But while I am a practitioner and an advocate of cyclical analysis, I am well aware that it probably won't achieve wide acceptance for a very long time to come.

Figure 11.11: All Ordinaries index—2007 market exit and 2009 entry points

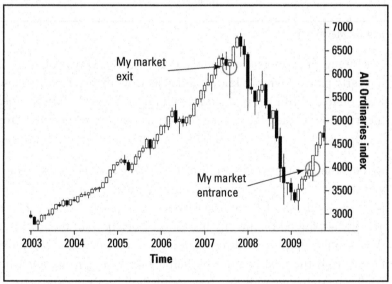

Source: MetaStock.

Mainstream investment mantra remains strongly centred on statistical analysis. The simple reality is that the vast majority of today's fund managers still employ modern portfolio theory, which was invented in the 1950s and is based almost entirely on the belief that market behaviour conforms to the normal distribution curve (or bell curve)—a commonly held, yet spurious, assumption I will take issue with in chapter 12.

Sadly, the only two forms of analysis that are compulsory learning for investment advisors today are fundamental analysis and modern portfolio theory. Even technical analysis, which has been in use for centuries, is still considered an optional topic in most training courses. The result is that only a handful of new-age boutique fund managers are prepared to employ cyclical analysis as part of their overall investment strategy—yours truly included.

You've no doubt heard the saying, 'It's time in the market, not market timing that counts'. This idea comes from the school of income investing and, as income investors generally don't sell their holdings and have little interest in the direction of price movements, it is quite valid. However, it certainly isn't a general rule of thumb—just ask anyone who was 100 per cent committed to the stock market throughout 2008 and see what they think of it as a global philosophy.

Market timing

Cyclical analysis is a blunt instrument, and it should never be seen as anything more than this. It can provide us with very broad market timing signals, but most, if not all, attempts to refine it any further will usually end in tears. Market timing using cyclical analysis allows us to predict future price direction and we human beings have a very powerful inclination to do this.

The advantage we have over other animals that share this planet with us is our ability to predict and anticipate the future. We have this ability because of our newer brain, the neo-cortex, and so we will always attempt to analyse, predict and anticipate. Whether it's wars, the weather, sporting endeavours, driving in traffic or financial markets—we will always try to predict and anticipate.

So is there a relatively simple and robust timing strategy that can help investors? Well I'm about to outline my approach to timing the market and, as you'll see, I use it only as a blunt instrument to tell me which overall strategy I should be employing at what time. The strategy could:

- rely on fundamental analysis
- rely on technical analysis
- invest in growth stocks
- hunt for income stocks
- move to cash and hedging.

My approach is based on understanding financial markets as complex adaptive systems, which is a very new science. It is an extension of chaos theory, a branch of mathematics first explored in the 1960s, but not popularised until the 1980s.

Rocket science

Before you read on, I must warn you that chapter 12 gives a reasonably detailed explanation of this science and how it applies to financial markets. Furthermore, there's no getting around the fact that it does get a little bit complicated and involved. It has to be included or else this discussion wouldn't be complete, but I have managed to corral all the rocket science into this one chapter.

If you're not overly interested in the nuts and bolts of understanding financial markets as complex adaptive systems and you just want to cut to the chase, then please skip over chapter 12. Chapter 13 explains how we apply this market understanding and all the practical implications of it, which is really what we, as investors, need to know.

But for those who do wish to study chapter 12, please be aware that some of the concepts and observations being introduced will have to be revisited (briefly) in chapter 13 for the benefit of those who do skip ahead. Anyway, whether you do or don't have any curiosity for this new science, I'm certain you will find its application to be an extremely powerful and invaluable tool.

Chapter 12

Financial markets as complex adaptive systems

Understanding financial markets as complex adaptive systems is all about getting a handle on how the broad market really works, as this is a prerequisite for successful market timing. And while I'd like to say that it is a simple matter to understand the underlying nature of financial markets, unfortunately we are about to enter the world of chaos theory and complex adaptive systems. But fear not: I will make every effort to maintain clarity when dealing with these somewhat esoteric topics. Let's start at the simplest point—the beginning.

Straight lines and curvy bits

The word *linear* essentially means straight line or straight line progression, and in order to simplify everything we see, humans have a profound tendency to view the world from a linear perspective. The main reason we want everything to be linear, or to progress in a straight line, is so we can both easily understand it *and* predict what is likely to happen in the future.

In more recent times, thanks largely to the power of modern computers, we have also pretty much mastered the ability to get our heads around curvy things as well. Of course, this is largely on the proviso that they are either constantly curvy or consistently changing, such as the case of an exponential curve, like the one shown in figure 12.1.

Figure 12.1: typical exponential curve

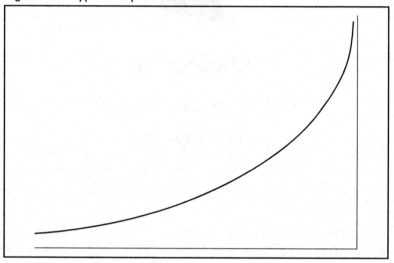

We can even project lines and curvy things into the future with a reasonably high degree of accuracy and determine if, when and where they're likely to intersect. The one proviso is that there aren't too many variables to consider.

But there's another problem that even the scientific community doesn't like to talk about, and that's the possibility of things changing but not doing so in a consistent way. In other words, the rate of change is not constant. It's bad enough that something can be dynamic (or changing) rather than static (thus rendering statistical analysis and the bell curve largely useless), but when the rate of change itself isn't linear or constant, then everyone starts to get a bit frightened. This is known as non-periodic behaviour, and it is shown in figure 12.2.

Figure 12.2: non-periodic behaviour

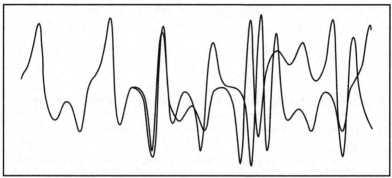

Source: Stewart I, *Does God Play Dice: The New Mathematics of Chaos,* Wiley-Blackwell UK, 1989, p. 141.

Let's sidetrack for a moment and look at the idea of a system being dynamic as opposed to static. Take the average life expectancy of the Australian population, for example. If you wanted to know the average number of years we're all expected to live then you would most likely use data from a recent 10-year period (see figure 12.3).

Figure 12.3: working out life expectancy using a 10-year period

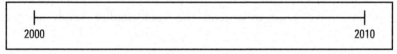

2000   2010

But what about using all recorded births and deaths over a 100-year period instead of just 10 years? Surely this larger sample of data will give us a more accurate and reliable answer (see figure 12.4).

Figure 12.4: working out life expectancy using a 100-year period

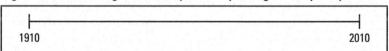

1910   2010

Put simply, no — because over this longer expanse of time factors that affect our lifespan, such as diet and medical advances, have changed significantly, making this sample period non-static and invalidating any averages taken. So let's go to the other extreme now and just use some very recent data. This should definitely give us the most up-to-date and accurate answer possible (see figure 12.5).

Figure 12.5: working out life expectancy using a one-year period

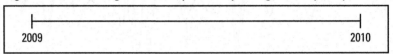

Unfortunately, we now have the problem of insufficient data to work with. This means that any sample of data that we subject to statistical analysis must be from a static system or a representative snapshot that allows for the dynamic nature of a system. Using the average lifespan of Australians over the past 10 years to reflect today's average is a snapshot approach and a compromise of sorts.

This is a pity, because everyone held out so much hope that statistical analysis was a universal solution for problems of randomisation. So the stock market, like other irregular phenomena, gets labelled as being unpredictable and that's that. Just like weather patterns, and even civilisation in general, the stock market simply has too many variables and is a dynamic system that's not always linear by nature. Figure 12.6 shows how the All Ords is forever changing its behaviour.

So people decide that, if we can't get our heads around a phenomenon, like the stock market, then it's random or so close to random it doesn't matter. Another neat way of dismissing things we can't fully comprehend or predict is by describing what's happening as noise, interference or turbulence. An engineer working in fluid dynamics, for instance, will most likely attempt to eliminate turbulent flow rather than try to understand it.

Figure 12.6: All Ordinaries index changing its behaviour over time

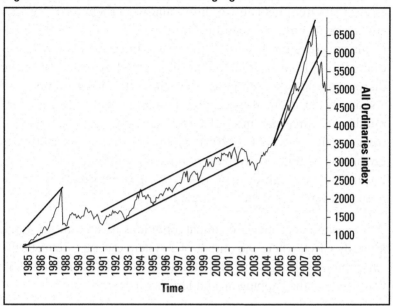

Source: MetaStock.

Introducing chaos theory

You can imagine the excitement about chaos theory when it first appeared back in the early 1960s, because it went a long way towards understanding what had previously been deemed as random phenomena. But the theory was largely dismissed by the broader scientific community at the time as a stream of pure mathematics without any real-world application. It was just a good excuse not to work on more practical stuff, like how to eliminate turbulence.

One of the first pioneers in the field of chaos theory was Edward Lorenz, a meteorologist trying to simulate weather patterns. At the beginning of the 1960s Edward had developed a set of 12 mathematical equations that he used to model real-world weather conditions, using a very early and (by current standards) very primitive computer system.

Like most experimenters Edward often repeated the same simulations over and over again to verify previous results. But on one occasion he had reason to pause a simulation that he had performed previously. To resume the process, Edward took a series of numbers from his latest printout and used them to re-seed his equations in order to continue from where he'd left off. Much to his surprise, the results of this interrupted simulation varied dramatically from his previous results. On close examination he discovered that the computer was internally using numbers to six significant decimal places, while his printout only gave him numbers to three significant decimal places. Hence a number that the computer saw as 0.152031 would be printed out as 0.152, giving a very minor discrepancy of just 31 millionths of one unit. But this was enough deviation to cause massive variations in the output of Edward's weather simulations.

This 'sensitive dependence on initial conditions' became known as the butterfly effect, where the output of a system can vary dramatically with minute changes in the starting conditions, comparable in magnitude to the flapping of a butterfly's wings:

> *The flapping of a single butterfly's wing today produces a tiny change in the state of the atmosphere. But over a period of time, the atmosphere actually does diverge from what it previously would have done. So, in a month's time, a tornado that would have devastated the Indonesian coast doesn't happen. Or maybe one that wasn't going to happen, does.*

This discovery and the work that followed led Edward Lorenz into the exciting new world of what is now known as chaos theory. While there is no commonly acknowledged fixed definition of what constitutes a chaotic system, it is generally accepted that the following conditions must be met:

- The system must be highly dependent on initial conditions.
- The system must employ at least two or more interacting variables.
- The initial conditions must be at least partially dependent on output (that is, iteration).

A good example of a chaotic system is the operation of a roulette wheel, which is probably best understood by analysing, step by step, the process of using one:

- An operator picks up a ball from a roulette wheel, which he or she then spins (the starting position of the wheel is dependent on where the ball landed after the previous operation—so the initial condition is dependent on the previous outcome).

- He or she then sets the ball rotating in the opposite direction (the wheel is the first variable whilst the ball represents the second variable).

- The ball eventually loses enough energy to drop into the spinning wheel (the outcome is extremely sensitive to the interaction of the two variables—the ball and the wheel moving in opposite directions).

Roulette is an excellent example of a two-variable chaotic system, which would in fact be predictable to a degree if a machine were used as the operator. It is actually the human operator that provides the random factor: but because the system is chaotic it can't be manipulated to any practical degree. Virtually all games of chance employ mechanisms or processes of a chaotic nature.

One of the other principal discoveries that Edward went on to make was that systems or models of systems behaving in a chaotic state produced repeating patterns that could be observed if the outputs were mapped in two dimensions, commonly referred to as *phase space* by chaoticians. Note that these repeating patterns are similar in form but never precisely identical. They typically produce patterns of nested, self-similar shapes like the Lorenz attractor, shown on the left of a typical price chart in figure 12.7 (overleaf).

Figure 12.7: Lorenz attractor (left) and a typical price chart (right)

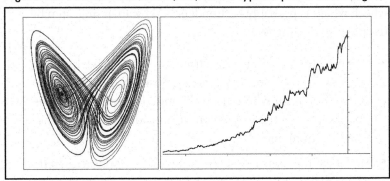

Source: MetaStock.

Chaos theory and financial markets

Any chart that shows the change in price with respect to time is a two-dimensional map, and if the stock market is a chaotic system of sorts, then anyone looking at price charts should observe nearly identical repetitive patterns. So here's the bit where it gets interesting and we jump back to financial markets.

It's time to introduce Benoit Mandelbrot, a mathematician working in a think-tank project for IBM during the early 1960s, primarily to solve the problem of noise on data transmission lines. However, Mandelbrot was also directed to investigate the nature of financial markets, obviously in the hope of the company being able to capitalise on any discoveries or developments that he might make.

Mandelbrot chose to study the price of cotton because he could obtain continuous data going all the way back to 1900. When he analysed the fluctuations in the price of cotton over half a century of market behaviour, the result was:

> *The numbers that produced aberrations from the point of view of normal distribution produced symmetry from the point of view of*

scaling. Each particular price change was random and unpredictable. But the sequence of changes was independent of scale: curves for daily price changes and monthly price changes were nearly identical. Incredibly, analysed Mandelbrot's way, the degree of variation had remained constant over a tumultuous sixty-year period that saw two World Wars and a depression.

Mandelbrot both identified a repeating pattern in the price activity and observed that it was nested, thus occurring at different levels of scaling (daily, weekly, monthly and so on). Furthermore, he confirmed the hopelessness of employing statistical analysis to study non-linear dynamic systems, like financial markets—hence our earlier discussion on the use of statistical analysis and how it is a compromise when applied to any type of dynamic system.

There are two key points worth noting. The first is that Mandelbrot's research should have placed a very serious question mark over the use of modern portfolio theory, which is anchored to the assumption that price deviation conforms to the normal distribution curve, when it doesn't.

As I stated in chapter 11, modern portfolio theory remains the most widely employed portfolio management approach in use today by fund managers around the world. Although it is terribly complicated and impressive, it simply doesn't work. If you follow financial news when markets experience a sharp correction you will no doubt have read a quote similar to this: 'According to our risk analysis models there was no possible way anyone could have predicted what was going to happen'. Straightaway you know their models employ the normal distribution (or bell) curve to explain market activity, shown in figure 12.8 (overleaf).

Figure 12.8: normal distribution (bell) curve

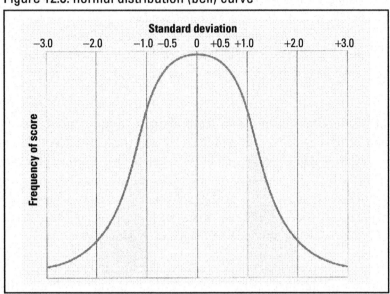

However — and here's the second point — Mandelbrot did state that markets were fractal in nature to some degree (*fractal* is a term Mandlebrot invented), because he observed self-similar patterns occurring at different levels of magnification. Hence, if you compare the weekly and monthly charts of the All Ordinaries in figure 12.9 you can see that the correction we experienced in 2007–08 wasn't entirely unpredictable when viewed from a fractal perspective.

These two charts of the All Ordinaries index are very nearly identical, even though they cover two entirely different time frames and periods. The first one is a weekly chart covering about five years of market activity from 1982 to 1987, while the second one is a monthly chart covering about 25 years of market activity from 1983 to 2008.

Figure 12.9: All Ordinaries index charts from a fractal perspective

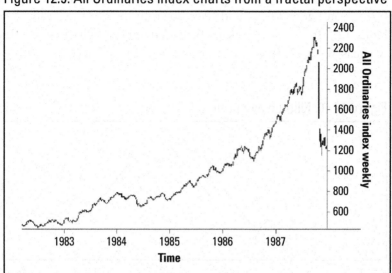

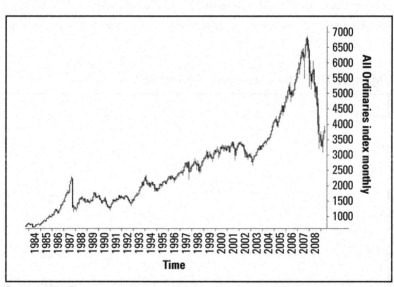

Source: MetaStock.

Mandelbrot had independently made observations that closely paralleled those of a famous technical analyst by the name of Ralph Elliott, father of the Elliott wave principle (EWP). EWP in its simplest form suggests that financial markets move up and down in a series of wave movements that can be quantified, an extension of Charles Dow's earlier work (see figure 12.10, overleaf).

Elliott's basic concept is that price activity moves up in five waves (1 to 5 on figure 12.10) and then down in three waves (a to c on figure 12.10). Waves 1, 3, 5 and b are said to be impulsive (upward), whereas waves 2, 4, a and c are referred to as corrective (down) waves.

Figure 12.10: Elliott wave principle

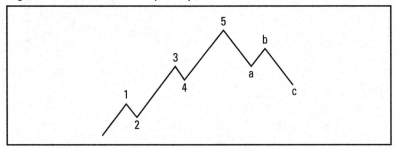

Elliott waves are nested (see figure 12.11), which means they are self-similar patterns occurring at different levels of magnification. Sound familiar?

Figure 12.11: Timbercorp chart—Elliott waves

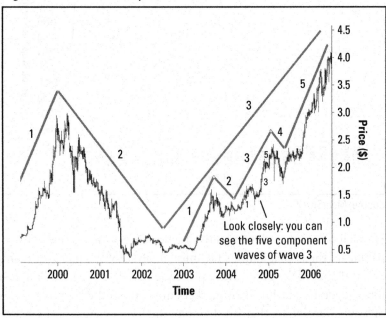

Source: MetaStock.

Unfortunately Elliott and his followers (commonly referred to as Elliotticians) promoted EWP as a universal solution to understanding financial markets, and so they have been largely ignored (and refuted) by the wider investment community. As we're about to see, techniques such as Elliott wave analysis are valid some of the time, but not all of the time.

Complex adaptive systems

The next problem we face in trying to understand the basic nature of financial markets is that while they seem to behave in a chaotic manner some of the time, they don't behave that way all of the time. So there isn't a single simple solution to understanding financial markets, as they appear to be constantly changing and adapting to external circumstances. You can see in figure 12.12 the clear contrast between the behaviour of the All Ordinaries in the 1980s compared to the 1990s.

Figure 12.12: All Ordinaries index showing different behaviour in the 1980s compared with the 1990s

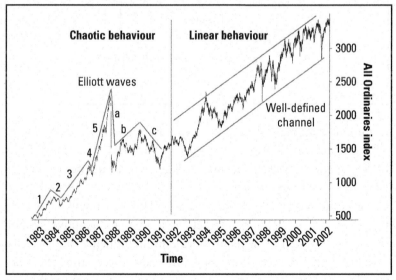

Source: MetaStock.

When markets are in a chaotic phase, they are best explained and modelled using techniques like Dow theory and the Elliott wave principle, and when they are in a linear phase then simple trendlines and conventional statistical analysis come to the fore. So there are times when modern portfolio theory does actually work.

While this discussion has come a long way in explaining the nature of the curvy bits (chaotic behaviour), we still have to figure out why the markets switch between making curvy bits and making straight lines. Fortunately, one of the latest developments in chaos theory is now able to provide an answer to this dilemma, with the introduction of what are commonly referred to as complex adaptive systems.

Put simply, a complex adaptive system (CAS) is a structure or process that is made up of independent yet freely interacting agents that react and adapt to external information or information feeding back from the system itself, or both. Well, I suppose it's not really all that simple, so maybe a diagram will help (see figure 12.13).

Figure 12.13: complex adaptive system

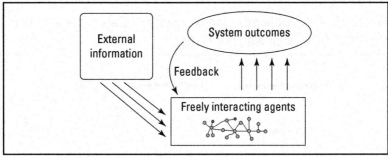

Common examples of complex adaptive systems include motor vehicle traffic, ant colonies, the ecosystem and even the human brain. Financial markets are also considered to be a type of complex adaptive system, where we can make the following substitutions in our generic diagram (see figure 12.14). This is a highly simplified representation of financial markets as a complex adaptive system, because we could include many more relevant influences and external variables, for instance. But using just these three straightforward parallels, the stock market as a complex adaptive system would look something like figure 12.15.

Figure 12.14: elements of a complex adaptive system applied to financial markets

External information	=> Company information, macro-economic factors, world events, and so on.
Freely interacting agents	=> Market participants—fund managers, investors, traders, speculators and so on.
System outcomes	=> Price movements caused by buying and selling among market participants.

Figure 12.15: the stock market as a complex adaptive system

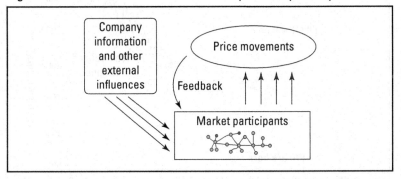

Market participants react to a combination of both external stimuli, such as company information, and feedback from the market itself, through price activity. When market participants are being strongly influenced by price activity (that is, internal feedback), the market is sentiment-driven and behaves largely in a chaotic manner.

But when external influences are the principal motivating force acting on participants, then the market moves away from this excited state, near the edge of chaos, and tends to behave in a more rational and predictable manner, very much in line with fundamental factors. The stock market as a complex adaptive system operates across a range of both rational and irrational states, and it's this behavioural spectrum that we want to understand more fully.

The behavioural spectrum

Let's go back to our chart of the All Ordinaries index showing the stock market operating at two distinctly different points on the behavioural spectrum. Going back to the beginning of the period shown would put us somewhere in the early stages of the 1980s stock market boom that began in 1982 (see figure 12.16).

Figure 12.16: the behaviour of the All Ordinaries index across two decades (1984–85)

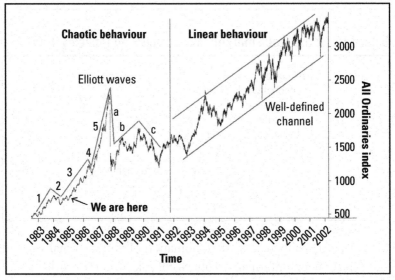

Source: MetaStock.

At this point the market has already enjoyed a good rally and is just getting set for another run up. Anyone who has owned shares for the past year or so is probably doing fairly well and would have a pretty good feeling about their stock market investments, thanks largely to the price of their holdings. We can highlight this phenomenon using the right-hand side of our complex adaptive system diagram (see figure 12.17).

Figure 12.17: stock market CAS—price feedback loop

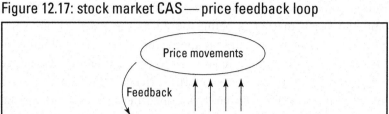

So while external factors, such as company fundamentals, are still worthy of consideration, there is no doubt the feedback from price activity is making market participants feel good. Of course they start to talk about how well they're doing to their friends, and the media plays its role in talking things up as well. In figure 12.18 we see the market experience another rally and the stock market, as a complex adaptive system, becomes even more lopsided in favour of price feedback.

Figure 12.18: the behaviour of the All Ordinaries index across two decades (1985–86)

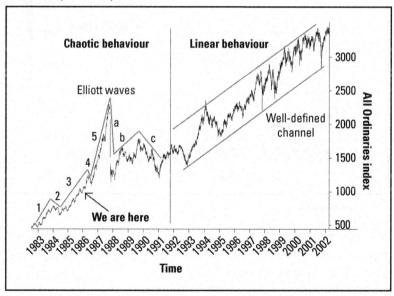

Source: MetaStock.

Anyone and everyone who owns shares is now doing very well, and the stock market is being touted as the place to be. Mind you, investors aren't talking about the financial wellbeing of the companies that they have an interest in so much as they're bragging about the increase in the price of their shares. As a result, investors become far less concerned about fundamental factors and totally preoccupied with price behaviour. And so the stock market as a complex adaptive system has now well and truly shifted towards the chaotic end of the spectrum, where the whole process is driven primarily by price feedback and there is little to no external influence governing investor behaviour. We find ourselves in an accelerating positive feedback loop (see figure 12.19).

Figure 12.19: the behaviour of the All Ordinaries index across two decades (1987)

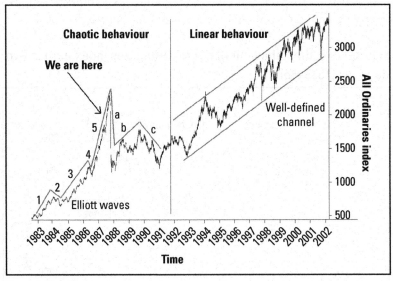

Source: MetaStock.

The system inevitably collapses, as price rises can't be sustained forever without the constant input of more and more energy (read: money), as shown in figure 12.20.

Figure 12.20: the behaviour of the All Ordinaries index across two decades (1987–88)

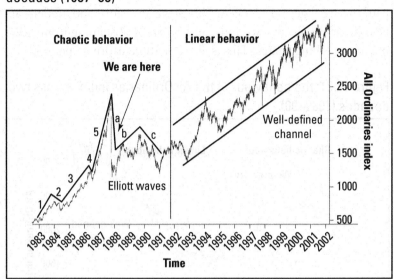

Source: MetaStock.

Note, too, that when the market moves up to the chaotic end of the spectrum, output and input become powerfully linked — investors wake up each morning and react to price activity from the day before and what overseas markets have done overnight. This is very much in keeping with one of the basic requirements of a chaotic system, where initial conditions are at least partially dependent on previous system outcomes (see our earlier discussion of chaos theory).

During this phase, where market participants are far more concerned with price activity than external factors, the market is sentiment-driven and you will note at times like these that share prices tend to move in unison. So when you look at intraday prices you will see that they are either all moving up together or down together. If you look at the ASX top 50 list on the ASX's website, all the share prices will be predominantly green or red — rarely an even mixture of both.

Now the market moves on to the consolidation phase, where market activity gradually narrows down over time, forming a crude triangular pattern (see figure 12.21). At this stage investors and traders are licking their collective wounds, and generally abstaining from either buying or selling shares. This is also a sentiment-driven period.

Figure 12.21: the behaviour of the All Ordinaries index across two decades (1989–90)

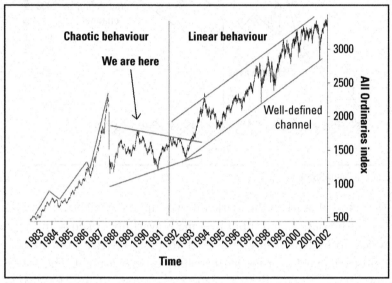

Source: MetaStock.

In figure 12.21 I have removed the markers for the a, b, c Elliott waves and replaced them with a pair of converging trendlines to better demonstrate how the market is consolidating over time. After a boom/bust cycle it is normal for many investors and traders to slowly leave the market and move on, causing this gradual reduction (or narrowing) in market activity. Of course, as with all things, the market won't stay in this subdued state forever and it will eventually begin to trend again, just as the All Ordinaries did from the early 1990s (see figure 12.22).

Figure 12.22: the behaviour of the All Ordinaries index across two decades (mid 1990s)

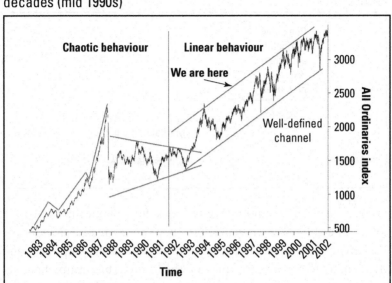

Source: MetaStock.

But something very significant happens as the market moves out of the consolidation phase and into another trending phase: it has completely changed its personality. Rather than galloping along at an unsustainable rate of about 25 per cent per year, as it did during the 1980s boom, it's now rising at a far more sustainable rate of about 9 per cent per year. In the particular case of the All Ords across the 1980s and 1990s, the shift from the chaotic end of the spectrum to a more subdued and rational state is well defined: hence the thin vertical line down the middle of all these charts.

It's no surprise that the fair-weather investors and high-flying speculators have all left the market in the hands of the more fundamentally motivated (and usually longer term) investors. This is a good time to revisit our stock market CAS diagram, which now operates in favour of external influences, where investors who rely largely on rational factors rule the day (see figure 12.23, overleaf).

Figure 12.23: stock market complex adaptive system — external factors rule

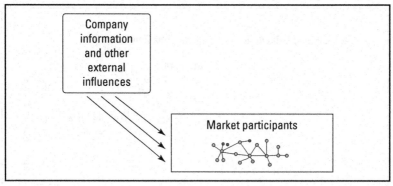

Longer term buy and hold investors care little about the short-term price behaviour of their shares, but they care a great deal about the underlying fundamentals of the companies the shares represent and their ability to generate income into the future. This group of market participants will actually buy more shares if the market drops in the short term and then sell them when they go too high, providing negative feedback as opposed to the positive feedback that we saw earlier during the boom phase.

So let's take a really big step back and look at a quarter of a century of market behaviour through the All Ordinaries index, shown in figure 12.24. You will note that the market appears to switch between rational and irrational states, thus repeating a very long term-cycle.

You will also note that the rational period lasted a great deal longer than either of the boom phases, and this makes sense, given that it takes far less energy to sustain a 9 per cent per year trend, driven by underlying fundamentals, than a 25 per cent per year rise during a boom phase.

In figure 12.24 I've defined the boom phases using two diverging trendlines. Chartists refer to these patterns as *speed resistance fans*.

Figure 12.24: All Ordinaries index cycling between rational and irrational states from 1983–08

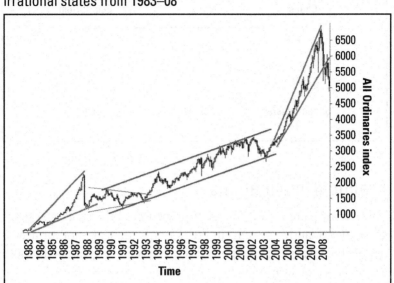

Source: MetaStock.

Now we come back to the behavioural spectrum, where we have chaos at one extreme and equilibrium at the other. But this time we can diagrammatically represent each state using chart patterns (see figure 12.25, overleaf). When a market is in a chaotic state, its behaviour can be defined by a speed resistance fan. When the market is in a rational state, it is operating in the middle part of the behavioural spectrum, and it can be defined by a channel with parallel boundaries. Finally, when it is consolidating or moving towards equilibrium, it can be defined by a triangle.

You can see how the stock market as a complex adaptive system moves up and down the behavioural spectrum, never quite reaching its limits or remaining close to either extreme for very long. Furthermore, we can identify where we are on this spectrum by defining the basic shape of the market progression as a speed resistance fan, channel or triangle.

Figure 12.25: behavioural spectrum and price patterns

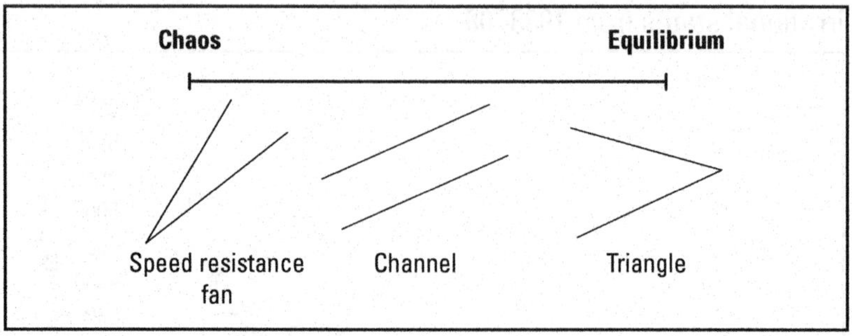

Practical implications

These chart patterns are emergent properties of the stock market as a complex adaptive system. In other words, they are not formed as the deliberate act of a few powerful investors or regulators, but as a consequence of swarm intelligence.

In a similar way, ant colonies are a complex adaptive system in which the ants always seem to put their food storage and waste materials at the opposite physical extremes of their nests. Scientists have examined this phenomenon closely and have deduced that it is a function of the group rather an inherent feature of individual ant behaviour. In other words, they haven't been able to teach individual ants to take out the rubbish, but when they get together in a group, they seem to magically figure it out for themselves.

But while this is a very elegant argument and makes for interesting reading, does it have any practical application? Well, as you're about to see in chapter 13, it has considerable practical implications, and while understanding financial markets as complex adaptive systems is still a very new science, even in its young and therefore relatively unrefined state, it is an invaluable investment tool.

Chapter 13

Using the right tactics at the right time

So it all comes down to this: using the right investment strategy at the right time. Chapter 11 introduced us to cyclical analysis and market timing, and I demonstrated how cyclical analysis is based on sound foundations and that it is the keystone to successful market timing. Then in chapter 12 we drilled down into the true nature of how financial markets work, which even included a crash course in chaos theory. But if all this understanding is to mean anything, then it needs to be applicable — and that's exactly what we're going to do right now: apply the theory to investing.

The important bits

Let's start by quickly reviewing the important bits from chapter 12 that have real-world applications, leaving the background detail (read: rocket science) behind. The discussion culminated with a simple diagram showing how the stock market operates on a behavioural spectrum, with chaos at one extreme and equilibrium or stillness at the other (see figure 13.1, overleaf).

The really important bit is that we can infer which part of the spectrum the stock market is operating in given the shape or pattern that the relative index is forming: a speed resistance fan (two diverging trendlines), a channel (parallel trendlines) or a triangle (converging trendlines).

As you will shortly see, knowing which part of the spectrum the market is operating in gives us a huge tactical advantage as investors.

Figure 13.1: behavioural spectrum and price patterns of the stock market

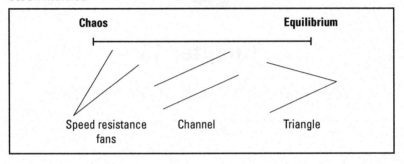

The other important bit we talked about in chapter 12 was that when the market is operating at either end of the behavioural spectrum, it is sentiment-driven. However, when it is operating in the middle of the spectrum, in its most rational state, investors are primarily motivated by fundamentals and other essentially logical factors. We can overlay this understanding on figure 13.1 to derive figure 13.2.

Figure 13.2: behavioural spectrum with an overlay of the main influences affecting the stock market

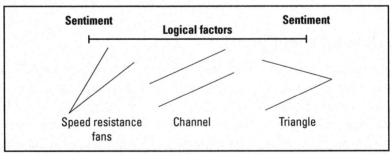

While the selection criteria for income stocks remain anchored heavily in fundamental analysis at all times, the tactics we employ to select growth shares can actually lean one of two ways. We can favour logical factors, on the basis that the market is operating in a rational state, or we can simply follow the crowd and buy into the shares that are getting all the attention—the current market darlings.

Fundamentals versus sentiment

In other words, we can primarily either employ fundamental analysis, or follow market sentiment by observing which shares are rising in price and getting all the publicity. This is probably a good place to introduce a working example, and a fairly illustrative choice would be the comparison of Fortescue Metals and Flight Centre.

We'll start with our recent boom which covered 2003 to 2006, when the rapid growth of China was the principal driving force and the Australian market, via the All Ordinaries, was best defined using a speed resistance fan. We were undoubtedly in a boom phase: the All Ords was rising at a rate of about 20 to 25 per cent per year and experiencing growing volatility (see figure 13.3). This was an exciting period that most investors, and indeed anyone who followed the news at the time, will well remember.

Figure 13.3: All Ordinaries index during the recent boom, defined by a speed resistance fan

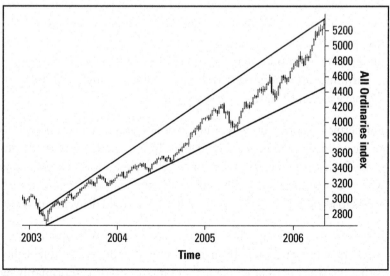

Source: MetaStock.

Now let's look at a chart of Fortescue Metals (FMG) over exactly the same period (see figure 13.4), showing its meteoric rise in price. In fact the price of Fortescue Metal's shares went up more than tenfold and continued to rise a lot further in the latter stages of the boom.

Figure 13.4: Fortescue Metals meteoric rise during the recent boom

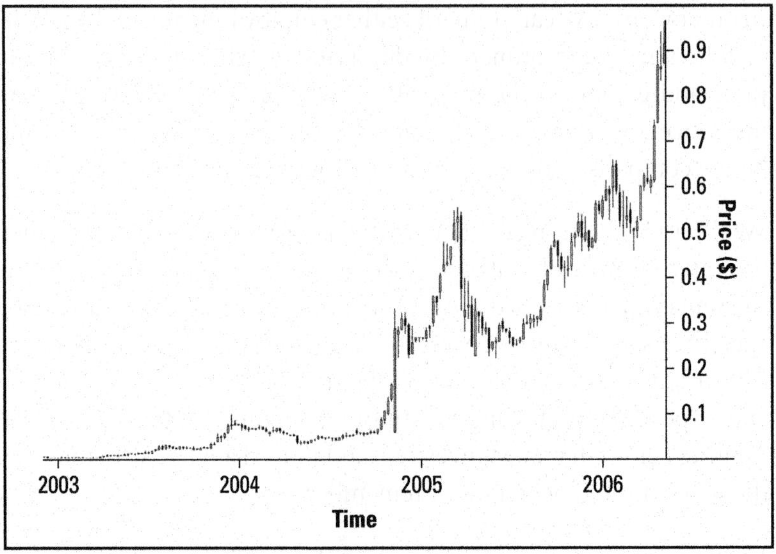

Source: MetaStock.

What makes this rather amazing is that Fortescue's balance sheet during this period was a sea of red. You couldn't actually say FMG had poor fundamentals, as the reality was that it effectively had *no* fundamentals. In other words, you couldn't even calculate its price-to-earnings ratio, because it didn't have any earnings. Mind you, it did have a cash burn rate — a scary one.

Furthermore, Fortescue was using new and unproven technology to surface-mine iron ore of a comparatively low grade compared with yields from more conventional mining techniques. It was in negotiations with potential buyers in China, while also trying to gain vitally needed access to its opposition's transport facilities so it could deliver its iron ore.

So to say that investing in Fortescue at the time was operating on hope and a prayer is probably a fair summation. But the simple reality is that the stock market was in a boom phase and driven primarily by sentiment. Fortescue had huge possibilities, was tied into the China story and its PR department was exceptionally good at making sure it appeared in the business news with monotonous regularity. Hence its share price went stratospheric, driven by market sentiment.

Now let's take a look at Flight Centre (FLT) which, unlike Fortescue, was a well-established business with a balance sheet that any CEO and board of directors would be proud of. Its return on equity, a fairly important financial ratio in anyone's book, remained in the range of 25 to 30 per cent per annum throughout 2003 to 2006. But FLT's price chart during the boom (see figure 13.5), covering exactly the same period as the two previous charts, shows its fall from grace.

Figure 13.5: Flight Centre during the recent boom

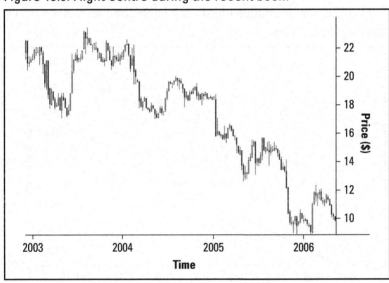

Source: MetaStock.

Flight Centre, a well-established business with sound fundamentals, had its share price cut in half during the same stock market boom — go figure. I do acknowledge there were lingering concerns about air travel after the September 11 terrorist attacks on the United States, and FLT was heavily invested in bricks-and-mortar retail outlets, which some investors felt were in danger of becoming obsolete.

But its key fundamentals and its earnings were clearly not in a state of decline during the period from 2003 to 2006. Quite simply, Flight

Centre wasn't tied to the China story, was a rather boring business with fairly predictable earnings, and therefore it was out of favour. The best thing the board of directors could have done to save the share price would have been to rename the company to Flight China or something similar.

And no, I'm not kidding, as this was the power of sentiment over fundamentals at the time. Go back to a period when fundamentals were in vogue, like the start of the new millennium, and it was an entirely different story. Figures 13.6 and 13.7 demonstrate how the All Ords was defining a channel (indicating a rational time) when Flight Centre's fundamentals obviously mattered to investors and they were driving its share price up.

Figure 13.6: All Ordinaries index defining a channel at the start of the new millennium

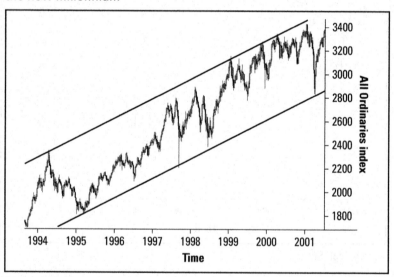

Source: MetaStock.

Figure 13.7: Flight Centre — rising share price

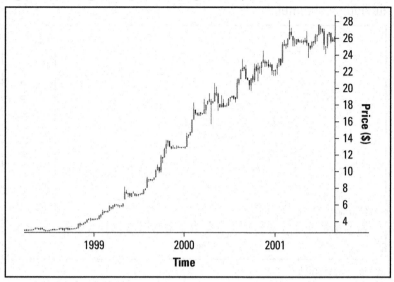

Source: MetaStock.

Choice of investment philosophy

It's also worth noting that your choice of managed fund will depend largely on what phase the market is in. During the 1990s, fund managers who sought out value using fundamental analysis would have done very well. However, these same fund managers would have stayed out of the market between 2003 and 2006 because share prices were rallying and so there was very little value to be found. Hence they would have been largely sidelined during the boom — not a good thing.

They were searching for undervalued shares when they should have been running with the crowd. So please be aware of the importance of understanding a managed fund's underlying investment philosophy and choosing the right philosophy at the right time. Nonetheless, markets do generally spend most of their time operating in a rational state (defining a channel) where fundamental analysis does play a key role and you will find value (see figure 13.8, overleaf).

Figure 13.8: the All Ordinaries index spends most of its time defining a channel

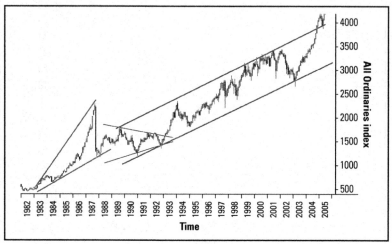

Source: MetaStock.

Extremes

Of course, by inference we also know that while markets will move to the extremes of the behavioural spectrum, it is typically only for a relatively short visit. In Australia our boom cycles tend to last about five years and our consolidation cycles are much the same, also about five years.

However, this is not the case for foreign markets, which all tend to run to the beat of their own drums. Figures 13.9, 13.10 and 13.11 (on p. 204) show examples of boom–bust–consolidation cycles from three different markets, from different historical periods and for different lengths of time

Figure 13.9: All Ordinaries index in boom–bust–consolidation

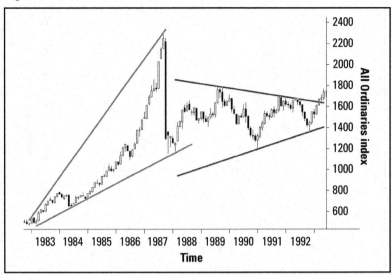

Source: MetaStock.

Figure 13.10: the Shanghai Composite index in boom–bust–consolidation

Source: MetaStock.

Figure 13.11: Dow Jones index in boom–bust–consolidation

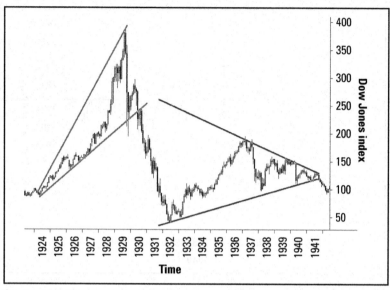

Source: MetaStock.

As you can see, boom–bust–consolidation cycles are a common phenomenon, and while there have been recent distortions of this pattern (which we'll look at shortly), it seems to be the natural order of things. Thus the stock market has a tendency, and indeed a preference, for being in the middle of its behavioural spectrum and, interestingly, this is a common feature of all complex adaptive systems. It has something to do with survival and, when you think about it, the rational state in the middle is really the safest place to be.

Staying in the middle

In fact, the rational state in the middle is so desirable that governments and key regulators are willing to do just about anything to keep us there. They talk up the economy and introduce stimulus when things slow down but discourage irrational exuberance during boom times. This is definitely the case in the United States, where I'm now going to take you on a historical tour of their stock market, via the Dow Jones index.

If you look back at figure 13.11 you'll note that it covers the boom–bust cycle of the roaring twenties and the subsequent consolidation period that lasted throughout the 1930s. On the assumption that stock markets are a fairly accurate depiction of the underlying business cycle and economy, what this consolidation period actually represents is the Great Depression. The 1930s was a time when the US economy was slowly grinding to a halt, and this was accurately reflected in the Dow Jones index. It was a painful period and one that the US government and economic regulators certainly never want to repeat. It is also worth mentioning that these periods of consolidation are actually more painful than the market crashes that precede them.

In a crash, a market will rapidly return to the level it was at some time earlier and, while it is a painful process, it is very much like tearing off a bandaid, as it's over fairly quickly. On the other hand, the subsequent consolidation period lasts for years and will inevitably impact everyone, and not just those who are directly exposed to the short-term fortunes of the market itself.

The thinking in the 1930s was that the current situation and recent demise of the stock market was directly attributable to rampant speculation, involving the use of debt and leverage. So both major political parties considered it appropriate economic policy to always return a budget surplus and operate well within their means, setting a solid example for the general populace. What this meant was that the government reduced its spending and imposed austerity measures—and inadvertently added to the pressures on an already fragile and slowing economy. But painful as it was, the US and the rest of the world did manage to come out the other side of the Great Depression, aided to some degree by the economic stimulation of the Second World War.

It wasn't until the early 1950s that the Dow Jones index managed to reclaim the highs it had reached during the peak of the boom in late 1929. It was somewhat paradoxical that for two long and tumultuous decades the US stock market underwent a very boring period as the Dow Jones defined a channel (being an overall rational period), as seen in figure 13.12 (overleaf).

Figure 13.12: Dow Jones index forming a channel, 1930s and 1940s

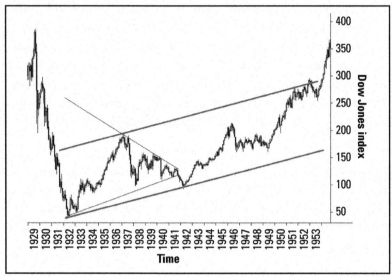

Source: MetaStock.

Then, at the start of the 1950s the stock market took off again in a postwar boom. Thus the whole cycle repeats itself, except this time the fun manages to last a little longer. Figure 13.13 shows the Dow Jones index across two boom phases, the 1920s, and the 1950s and 1960s.

Figure 13.13: Dow Jones index, 1920s to 1960s

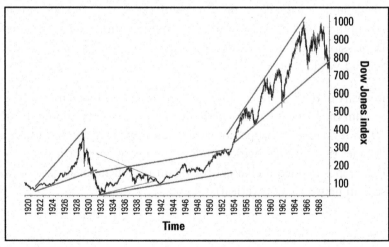

Source: MetaStock.

However, this time there's been a subtle change as the somewhat radical and new age ideas of John Maynard Keynes, a British economist, have started to take hold on a global scale. Keynes was born in 1883 and died in 1946, just before his macroeconomic theories influenced government policy around the world, mainly in the United States and in the United Kingdom.

Keynes's theories and ideas led to a school of economic thought that bears his name — Keynesian economics. At the core of Keynesian economics is the idea that governments and key economic regulators can manipulate the economy and business cycles in order to keep them operating at peak efficiency. For example, it would be impossible for an economy to operate at peak efficiency without full employment, or close to it. Thus a government could create employment by undertaking public works, and regulators could reduce interest rates to free up money supply, which would encourage the private sector to expand and also employ more workers.

Keynes believed that economies should be stimulated in order to keep them operating as efficiently as possible, which would help to ensure that a disaster like the Great Depression would be avoided in the future. Curiously, this revolutionary thinking first came about in the 1930s, but wasn't widely adopted until the 1950s.

The global economy, with the exception of Europe, enjoyed a postwar boom, where some of the credit for the general prosperity was attributed back to the implementation of Keynesian economic measures. However, the real test came when the postwar boom finally ended in the late 1960s and the next corrective phase began. But this time we don't see a consolidation pattern occur in the Dow Jones index, as we would normally expect. In fact, a widening pattern occurs, as can be clearly seen in figure 13.14 (overleaf).

Figure 13.14: Dow Jones index, 1950s to 1970s

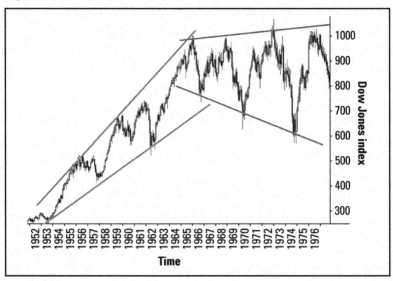

Source: MetaStock.

The United States completely moved away from the gold standard in the late 1960s, which gave the government the freedom to manipulate the value of US currency—and even print more money in order to stimulate the domestic economy. In August 1971, John Connolly, the then secretary of the US Treasury in the Nixon administration, announced a series of stimulus measures, which included both quantitative easing (read: printing money) and the lowering of interest rates.

So it would appear that employing Keynesian economic measures did allow the United States to avoid a repeat of the Great Depression—a period of consolidation and economic contraction that normally follows a boom–bust cycle. What did occur was a sideways channel with a bulge in it that lasted for about 17 years. Figure 13.15 is a chart of the Dow Jones index spanning the 1960s to the 1980s, showing this prolonged sideways period.

Keynesian economics may have prevented an economic contraction, but it appears to have created a grinding secular bear market in its place. (A secular bear market is one that undergoes a series of major upswings and downswings but ultimately moves sideways or lower.) It's an interesting trade-off and one that was to finally bring Keynesian economics into question. It would appear that stimulating an economy is similar to an athlete using steroids: short-term enhancement for long-term deterioration.

Figure 13.15: Dow Jones index, 1960s to 1980s

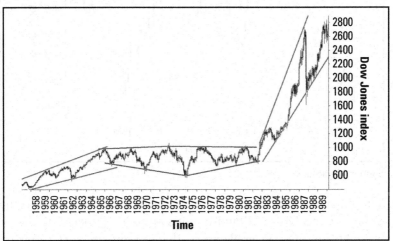

Source: MetaStock.

Nonetheless, this real-world example does illustrate the powerful desire of a government and key regulators to keep the economy away from the extremes of the behavioural spectrum by just about any means possible. These were powerful stimulus measures that received a lot of criticism from both leading economists of the day and key US trading partners. But was this purely about economic survival or were there other agendas at work as well?

An amazing coincidence

To answer this question, let's go back to John Connolly's announcement of a stimulus package in 1971, which I believe has a powerful connection to what's happening in the United States in 2012. The time of the release of this stimulus package is marked in figure 13.16 (overleaf) with a small circle. In this chart of the Dow Jones I've zoomed in on the widening pattern that was occurring across the late 1960s and early 1970s.

Figure 13.16: Dow Jones index, late 1960s to early 1970s

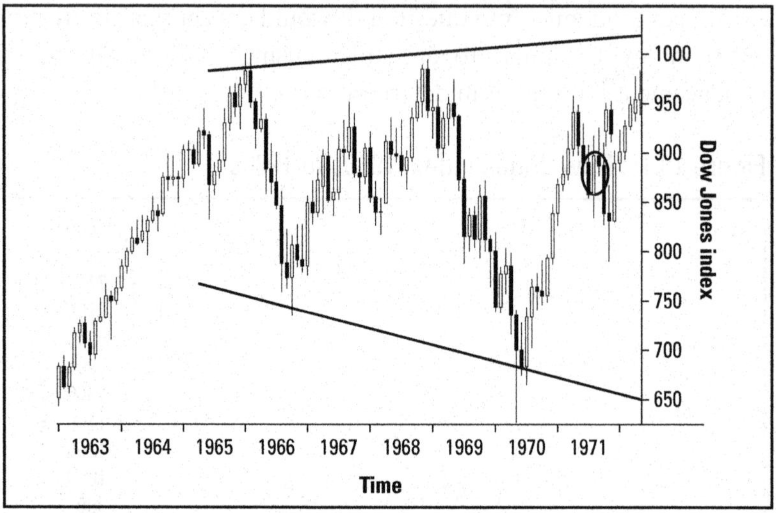

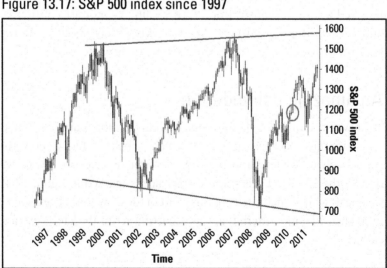

Source: MetaStock.

What makes this chart extremely interesting, along with the timing of the Nixon administration's stimulus package, is that it bears an uncanny resemblance to the current situation. Compare figure 13.16 of the Dow Jones in the late 1960s and early 1970s with the current chart of the S&P 500 in figure 13.17, where I've circled the US Federal Reserve's recent announcement of quantitative easing in 2010 (commonly referred to as QE2).

Figure 13.17: S&P 500 index since 1997

Source: MetaStock.

Although these two charts cover completely different time frames, the two patterns are incredibly similar. What's more, the timing of the stimulus packages also coincide with one another, suggesting not only a technical parallel but also a strong fundamental connection too.

But wait, there's more because now I'm going to show you a third similarity. Remember in chapter 11 we looked at the US political cycle and the pattern that emerged when we filtered out only the US presidential elections where the incumbent was sitting for re-election (see figure 11.6, on p. 164)? Well, interestingly, President Nixon was running for his second and final term of office in November of 1972, which perfectly coincides with the peak of the cycle in the US stock market. The chart of the Dow Jones index in figure 13.18 has a circle around November 1972, the time of the US presidential election.

Figure 13.18: Dow Jones index showing the 1972 US presidential election

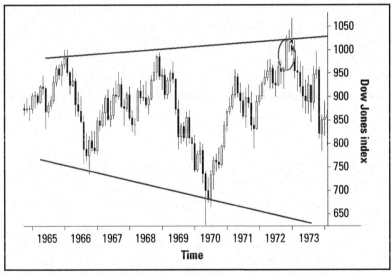

Source: MetaStock.

Now let's take a look at the current situation in 2012. When we project the long-term trend in the S&P 500 all the way to the upper boundary, the two lines intersect in late 2012. This can be clearly seen in figure 13.19 (overleaf) and no prizes for guessing when the forthcoming US presidential election is due: in November 2012 President Barack Obama will be running for his second term in office.

Figure 13.19: current S&P 500 projected to the upper boundary

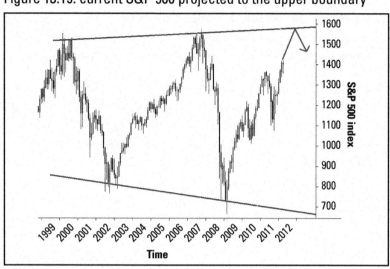

Source: MetaStock.

So is there a slim possibility that Keynesian economics has been hijacked by self-interested politicians? I guess you'd have to be a bit cynical to think that was the case—call me a cynic.

Now, to project into the future let's take a look at how the situation played out after the 1972 presidential election. Figure 13.20 shows the dramatic decline of the Dow Jones during 1973 and 1974 to levels not seen since the early 1960s.

Figure 13.20: decline of the Dow Jones index in 1973 and 1974

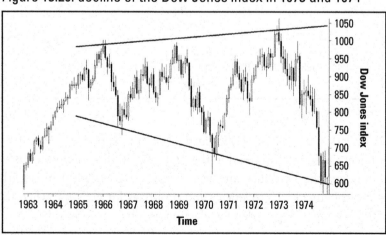

Source: MetaStock.

Figure 13.20 strongly suggests that, as investors, we should be exercising extreme caution from the end of 2012, as a major decline in the US markets in 2013 and 2014 is a very distinct possibility. Figure 13.21 paints a very bleak picture if indeed the US stock market follows the same path as it did 40 years ago.

Figure 13.21: forecast of the S&P 500 cycling down in 2013 and 2014

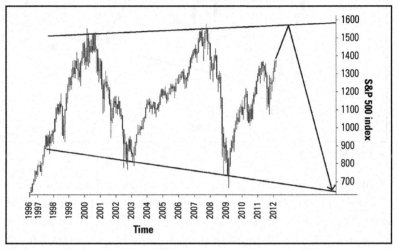

Source: MetaStock.

I'll be watching for signs of a major market reversal if and when the S&P 500 does reach its upper boundary, and will warn my subscribers accordingly. As you may recall from chapter 11, I recommended getting out of the market in late 2007 and not returning until mid 2009. I actually consider this a far more obvious cycle than the decline of 2008 and therefore one that will be easier to anticipate.

The local economy

Closer to home, our government certainly isn't guilty of employing stimulus to avoid a contraction of our stock market and underlying economy. Figure 13.22 (overleaf) shows that we are currently repeating the same consolidation cycle we went through after the 1987 crash.

Figure 13.22: the All Ordinaries index contracting since 2009

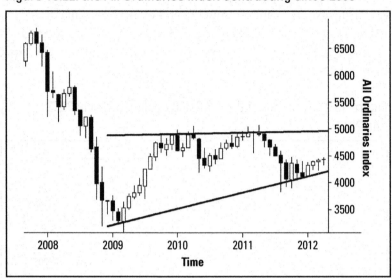

Source: MetaStock.

Right now, in mid 2012, our government has introduced a carbon tax and a mining tax, and is doing everything in its power to deliver a budget surplus. These are all austerity measures that will work to slow the economy. Our government's actions are just a little bit odd considering the circumstances and the fact that the rest of the world is largely moving in the opposite policy direction.

So could the federal government be acting out of self-interest by appeasing the Australian Greens Party and saving their pennies for the 2013 budget, which is just before the next federal election? Regardless of the motivation, I find it highly contradictory for our federal treasurer to repeatedly declare himself a devout believer in Keynesian economics when his actions and the government's economic policies clearly lean in the opposite direction.

While I may appear to be veering away from the topic of market timing, this type of broad-based discussion does help to illustrate the interconnection between politics, macroeconomics, the business cycle and, ultimately, financial markets. However, we will now move on to the more practical aspects of how to interpret and respond to market behaviour.

Growth, income or cash

This is the easy bit: if we know what phase and which part of the cycle our market is in, then knowing what tactic(s) to apply is fairly straightforward. We'll start with the period in early 2009 that is circled in figure 13.23, showing the All Ordinaries index.

Figure 13.23: All Ordinaries index (a circle indicates early 2009)

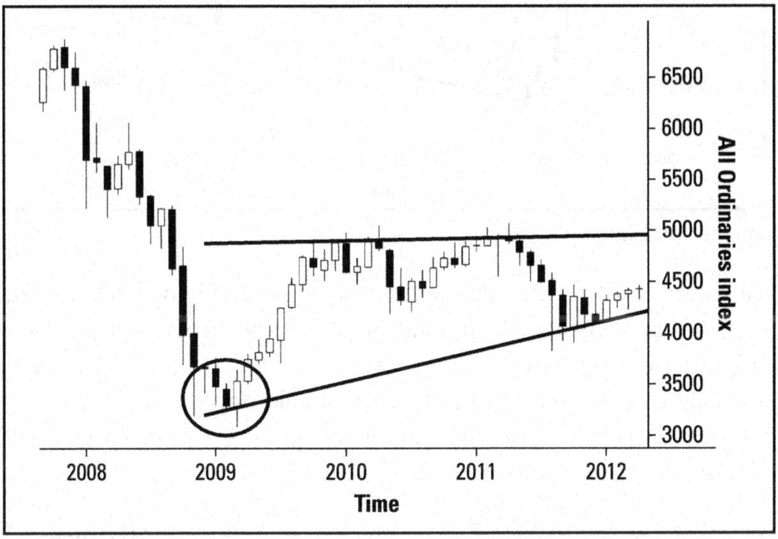

Source: MetaStock.

Early 2009 was a major low point in the recent market cycle and it certainly wasn't a good time to be exposed to growth stocks. At that time my growth portfolio was completely in cash and I was on the hunt for potential income stocks, in accordance with the discussion we had in chapter 9, where I demonstrated how the list of potential asset-class shares in my newsletter was overflowing with opportunities in March of 2009.

On the other hand, when the market has moved away from its low point and is rallying up, then hunting for income stocks is off the agenda and we want to be exposed to growth stocks. In figure 13.24 (overleaf) of the All Ords, I've circled mid 2009, when I recommended buying back into growth shares.

Figure 13.24: All Ordinaries index (a circle indicates mid 2009)

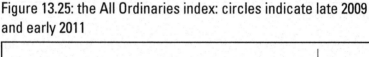

Source: MetaStock.

However, it wasn't long before I recommended moving back to cash, as the market began to hesitate in late 2009. In fact, caution was the order of the day in both late 2009 and early to mid 2011. These were times to be mainly out of growth stocks and not looking to buy income stocks either, as the market was at a high point in its cycle. These periods are both circled in figure 13.25.

Figure 13.25: the All Ordinaries index: circles indicate late 2009 and early 2011

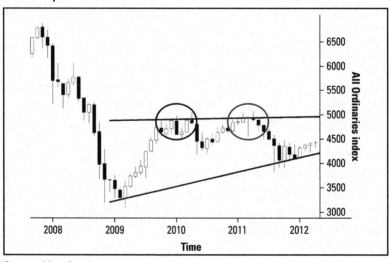

Source: MetaStock.

But then the market cycled down again, forming another major low in August 2011. And, as before, this was a time to be completely out of growth stocks, but on the lookout for potential income stocks. This period is circled in figure 13.26, showing the All Ordinaries index.

Figure 13.26: All Ordinaries index (a circle indicates August 2011)

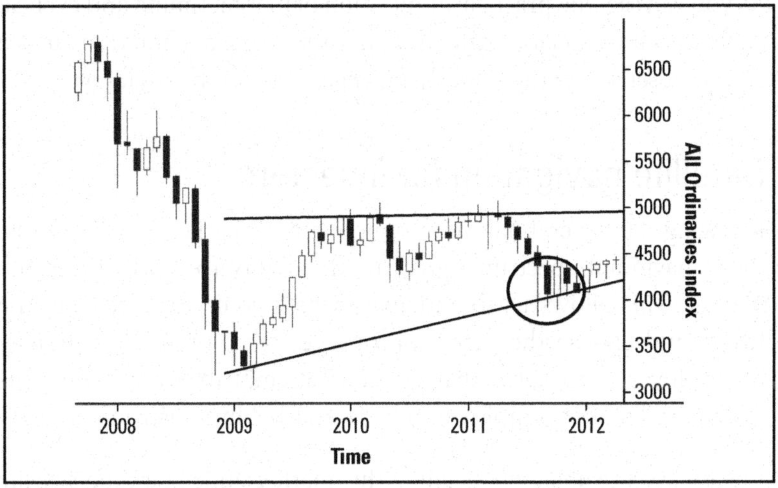

Source: MetaStock.

An even simpler application of this market understanding is to use it as a cash switch. Investors who don't actually own shares directly but prefer to use managed funds will find this approach particularly useful. All we do is vary the amount of money we have exposed to the market through managed funds versus the amount of money we have in cash.

Table 13.1 shows my recommendations for the different moments in the recent market cycle.

Table 13.1: a recommended proportion of managed funds versus cash for 2009 to 2011

Time	Managed funds	Cash
March 2009	0%	100%
Mid 2009	80%	20%
Late 2009 and mid 2011	20%	80%
Late 2011	80%	20%

By late 2011 the markets were beginning to turn up again and so I would have increased my exposure to funds. Note that I never recommend being 100 per cent exposed to managed funds, as I would always want to have a cash reserve to draw on in case I need money quickly.

As you can see, the practical application of market timing and cyclical analysis is a reasonably straightforward process, anchored in simple common sense. It's the underlying analysis that's the tricky bit!

Satellite navigation for investors

Knowing the general nature of how financial markets work (that is, the behavioural spectrum) gives us the ability to model the stock market. This allows us to anticipate what's going to happen in the future and choose the most appropriate (read: profitable) strategy to employ. The caveat is that we don't attempt to overly refine this insight and that we employ it only as a fairly blunt instrument.

I really like the analogy of calling this market understanding *satellite navigation for investors*. It points us in the right direction, but if we just blindly follow it with total faith then we could end up driving into the sea. I personally drive with most of my attention on the road in front of me and my surroundings, occasionally glancing at the SatNav map to reassure myself I'm still heading towards my desired destination.

The strategies described for finding and managing growth and income shares in parts II and III of this book are the roads we can take, and the market timing techniques in part IV tell us which road we should be on at what time. To create and preserve real wealth we must employ the right tactics at the right time.

Also, as I have demonstrated in parts of this discussion, the precepts of market timing are built on shifting sands, as political winds and macroeconomic policies are constantly changing. This is very much a topical subject and so my *Blue Chip Report* (see the appendix on p. 227) includes a regular weekly update of my latest market analysis and recommendations.

Chapter 14

Plan to take action

By the time the cameras actually start to roll on a film set, the bulk of the work has already been done. The screenplay has been finalised; the funding has been raised; the cast and crew have been selected and assembled; the sets and costumes are all made—and a whole lot more. It's expensive, complicated and time consuming, and would be impossible to orchestrate without a very detailed and thorough master plan.

The planning phase has been undertaken by the production team long before anything else is actually done. In the same vein, investors need to create a master plan before they buy a single share. Having a plan is the keystone of good organisation. Good planning is a forerunner to good organisation, and good organisation is an essential component for success in any field.

Organisation

In the 1970s a university study attempted to uncover the secret to success, whether it be success of an academic nature, in a sporting arena or in the commercial world. The researchers interviewed successful people of all ages and from different walks of life to try to identify any common factors.

Much to their surprise it wasn't IQ, natural talent, how hard they worked, how much money they started with or which social stratum the successful person belonged to. All of these were certainly contributing factors, but the common key to success was, you guessed it, organisation.

But this is rhetoric that you've probably come across somewhere before, which isn't really surprising since it's been around in one form or another for at least 2500 years. Pythagoras, the famous mathematician who was born in 570 BC and died in 495 BC (approximately), instructed his students and devoted followers to repeat the following verse when rising from their daily slumber:

As soon as you awake, in order lay

the actions to be done the coming day

But thorough planning and good organisation are totally useless unless it leads to action:

Allow not sleep to close your eyes

before three times reflecting on

your actions of the day. What deeds

done well, what not, what left undone.

These are more teachings from Pythagoras, whom I think could be accurately described as a successful individual, albeit one who lived 2500 years ago. So while this book contains a wealth of information for the DIY investor, reading it will count for nothing unless you plan to take action and then act on your plan. Now you probably think I'm going to lay out the entire blueprint for a successful investment strategy—but I'm not.

We're all different

The only plan I can write is my own, and that one is written. However, my plan is not generic and so there's little point in sharing it with you, because we're all different and so we all need a different overall strategy. All I can really do is raise some of the more obvious issues that you are likely to encounter and address these. We'll start with the simple question of how much time you have.

Time is precious

We all pay for our ambitions in the common currency of time: those with modest ambitions, relative to their net worth, will have more time to spare than those of us who want to reach for the stars. Thus a capital base of $500 000 and a very modest lifestyle costing $50 000 per year or less means that quitting your daytime job could be just around the corner. On the other hand, realising an objective of an income of $150 000 per year will be considerably further down the track.

The other variable that comes into play here is that some of us have more time than others. When I was 30 years old I could afford to be very ambitious, as I had a large proportion of my life ahead of me. Now I'm 50 and I have less time ahead of me, and so my time is becoming more precious. My ambitions are slowly coming into line with my current net worth as I gradually get older. Financial over-ambition later on in life is dangerous, because we don't have the time to undo any damage. Of course, the flip side of this is that to not take action when you're younger is to simply waste your time.

For a younger person who does have plenty of time, to not invest is to take a risk. So no action does not necessarily equate to no risk—a point not often made. Our time is precious and shouldn't be wasted, or foolishly risked. Remember that it is possible to replace money, which flows in both directions, but it's not possible to replace time—clocks move in only one direction.

Aversion to risk

The time–money equation is one that we must all address individually, along with how much risk we can comfortably live with. The final equation actually has three variables: time, money and risk. There's no point in being exposed to investments that prevent you from getting a good night's sleep: you'll simply shorten your time by having a heart attack.

I have a fairly low aversion to risk and sleep quite well most of the time. But there are others who would toss and turn all night long if they were exposed to my investment portfolio. Here, once again, we are all different and so there is no one-size-fits-all approach possible when it comes to investment solutions.

Once we've analysed our individual circumstances by asking ourselves how much money is enough, how precious is our time and how much risk can we comfortably stomach, then we can start to draw up a basic map of how we are going to invest in shares. There are essentially two primary questions that we must address: how much of your total net worth are you going to invest in shares; and what is your capital allocation to growth shares versus income shares going to be?

Mutually exclusive

This brings me to another question I get asked a lot: are growth shares and income shares mutually exclusive? Answer—well, not really, but it's best to treat them that way. Growth shares earn profits and pay dividends, while income shares will often enjoy a rising share price—the good ones anyway.

I have a growth portfolio with its own separate pool of money and trading account, and an income portfolio with its own trading account. This not to say that you can't move shares between these two portfolios or even own the same share in both portfolios.

Back in chapter 10, as part of the discussion of the ongoing management process for income stocks, I demonstrated, with a working example, a situation where I would have transferred a share from my income portfolio across to my growth portfolio. And shares can move the other way as well.

Take the case of Commonwealth Bank (CBA) during the late 1990s, when its share price eventually stopped rising, but its dividend payouts continued to increase. Figure 14.1 shows how CBA was an attractive growth proposition until late 1999, when its share price began to move sideways.

Although its share price began to slow, CBA's half-yearly dividend payouts continued to trend up, and if it had been held for some time then it would have been an attractive income stock by late 1999.

Figure 14.1: CBA share price trend, late 1990s

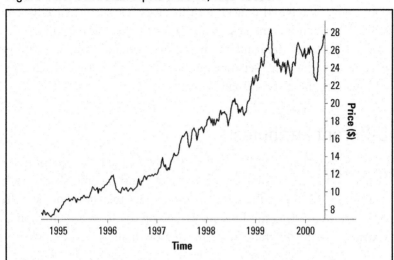

Source: MetaStock.

It could, therefore, have legitimately been moved across to an income portfolio. Now we'll take the example of CBA a step further by jumping forward to when it was rising in price again from 2004 to 2007, as seen in figure 14.2.

Figure 14.2: CBA share price trend early in the new millennium

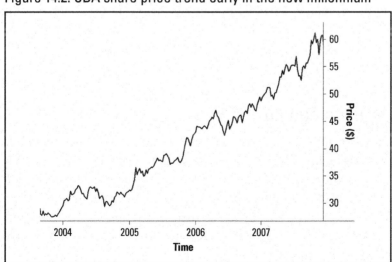

Source: MetaStock.

So once more it would have made an attractive growth share and we could have purchased it again on this basis. We would have owned CBA as both an income share and a growth share at the same time. This is a perfectly valid and not uncommon situation where investors need to view these two separate holdings as being mutually exclusive, and manage them accordingly.

Different attributes

Now as you may recall, I have already tackled the question of how to split one's capital between growth and income shares back in chapter 10. I listed a series of key points that investors should consider when deciding how they're going to allocate their capital, highlighting the different attributes of growth and income stocks.

Where these types of stocks differ considerably is with respect to time and risk: growth stocks take more time to manage, and represent greater risk. So one would expect that an older investor, whose time is becoming very precious, would be inclined to allocate more of their capital to income stocks than growth shares.

The amount of capital we allocate to each portfolio will once again depend on our individual circumstances and nature. Although there is often another complication: how do we manage our existing holdings? In other words, when we turn over a new leaf as investors, we are often faced with the initial dilemma of what to do with the shares we already own.

Housecleaning

People who have inherited shares often ask me what they should do with them. My usual response is that, given that they were effectively obtained for free, their dividend yield (assuming they pay any sort of a dividend) is infinity per cent. This immediately qualifies them as income shares, and given that there is less opportunity to acquire income shares than growth shares, my preference would be to add them to my income portfolio.

I refer to this process of sorting out one's existing holdings as housecleaning. Of course, some of the shares we already own will obviously fall into the category of growth shares, while others will easily qualify as income or asset-class shares. But the hard part of this process is having to bite the bullet and sell any shares that don't belong in either category.

Next, we need to decide how we're going to manage the shares that we are going to keep. Managing income shares is a fairly universal process, as described back in part III, but growth shares are a slightly different matter. We need to implement a suitable trading strategy, like the one described in part II, but you may find that it's not quite appropriate for your existing holdings.

The stop loss may be too tight at 20 per cent drawdown, or your shares may not be rising fast enough to meet the minimum requirement of 25 per cent per year. But whatever you decide to do, remember that applying a trailing stop loss is the single most critical aspect to any growth management strategy. Of course, all these recommendations count for nothing if we don't implement them.

Take action

The tools for financial freedom are at our disposal — we simply have to decide to take action. Those who will succeed are those who take action, not those who have read more books and been to more seminars. Having an abundance of knowledge will not protect us from financial loss, and neither will leaving our money in the bank, where we suffer a loss of opportunity instead.

This book is an instruction manual on how to invest in shares, but it is nothing more than interesting reading material unless you choose to take action. Pretty much everything I know about investing in shares is contained in these pages and it is knowledge that I have accumulated through decades of market experience. It is the result of my actions and I sincerely hope it becomes the incentive for yours.

Appendix:
Blue Chip Report 10-year
simulation results

Blue Chip Report simulation

As this is a conditional simulation these results should be treated as an approximate guide only. Bear in mind the following:

- Starting capital is $100 000 and brokerage and dividends are both ignored.

- All trades use the opening price just after the buy or sell signal is given.

- If no Sell Price ($) is shown then the share was held at the end of the simulation.

- For the sake of simplicity, profit taking at 15 per cent of total capital is ignored.

- Alan's monthly commentary (introduced in September 2006) is also ignored.

July 2001 to June 2002

Code	Number of shares	Buy price ($)	Value at purchase ($)	Value at sale/end ($)	Sell price ($)
VSL	2824	3.54	10 000	7 286	2.58
TOL	2053	4.87	10 000	16 260	
SGN	2732	3.66	10 000	8 606	3.15
WES	416	24.03	10 000	10 492	25.22
CXP	2247	4.45	10 000	9 707	4.32
ORG	3436	2.91	10 000	11 270	
SUN	675	14.80	10 000	7 830	11.60
COH	257	38.90	10 000	10 460	40.70
WOW	933	10.71	10 000	12 269	
PPT	250	39.96	10 000	10 725	
RHC	1963	3.71	7 286	8 127	

(continued)

July 2001 to June 2002 (*cont'd*)

Code	Number of shares	Buy price ($)	Value at purchase ($)	Value at sale/end ($)	Sell price ($)
MIG	3023	2.59	7830	7890	2.61
LEI	910	9.45	8606	9455	
CSL	214	45.38	9707	9157	42.79
HSP	4798	2.18	10460	11803	
UTB	2609	3.51	9157	9914	
BLD	2690	3.90	10492	10087	
MGW	1631	4.80	7830	7666	
VSL	2824	3.54	10000	7286	2.58
TOL	2053	4.87	10000	16260	
SGN	2732	3.66	10000	8606	3.15

Total number of trades = 8

Win–loss ratio = 11 wins to 7 losses (61%)

Final capital at 30 June 2002 = $107576 (up 7.6%)

S&P/ASX 200 index = down 7.9%

July 2002 to June 2003

Code	Number of shares	Buy price ($)	Value at purchase ($)	Value at sale/ end ($)	Sell price ($)
TOL	1259	7.94	10000	9254	7.35
HSP	4049	2.47	10000	8989	2.22
RHC	2364	4.23	10000	9314	3.94
MGW	2128	4.70	10000	8938	4.20
BLD	2667	3.75	10000	11388	4.27
UTB	2632	3.80	10000	16318	
LEI	965	10.36	10000	9225	9.56
WOW	767	13.03	10000	8751	11.41
FWD	3472	2.88	10000	13992	
CDO	3571	2.80	10000	9606	2.69

Code	Number of shares	Buy price ($)	Value at purchase ($)	Value at sale/ end ($)	Sell price ($)
ALS	2391	3.87	9254	9444	3.95
WYL	2910	3.20	9314	10185	
ORI	877	9.98	8751	7498	8.55
ANN	1192	7.50	8938	7748	6.50
GUD	2534	3.64	9225	12087	
GNS	4501	2.53	11388	13053	
CTX	3695	2.60	9606	10752	

Cash on hand as at 30 June 2003 due to lack of shares available = $34932

Total number of trades = 7

Win–loss ratio = 8 wins to 9 losses or 47%

Final capital as 30 June 2003 = $111319 (up 11.3%)

S&P/ASX 200 index = down 5.8%

July 2003 to June 2004

Code	Number of shares	Buy price ($)	Value at purchase ($)	Value at sale/ end ($)	Sell price ($)
GNS	3448	2.90	10000	11378	
GUD	2079	4.81	10000	17983	
FWD	2469	4.05	10000	19011	
UTB	1612	6.20	10000	13315	
CTX	3424	2.92	10000	29400	
FKP	3921	2.55	10000	10744	
SGM	990	10.10	10000	11355	
ALN	1633	6.12	10000	9341	5.72
BLD	1811	5.52	10000	9218	5.09
QBE	995	10.05	10000	12935	
MGQ	3245	2.84	9218	10903	
NCM	815	11.45	9341	11532	

Total number of trades = 2

Win–loss ratio = 10 wins to 2 losses or 83%

Final capital as 30 June 2003 = $148556 (up 48.6%)

S&P/ASX 200 index = up 16.8%

July 2004 to June 2005

Code	Number of shares	Buy price ($)	Value at purchase ($)	Value at sale/ end ($)	Sell price ($)
CTX	1116	8.96	10000	17689	
CIY	2288	4.37	10000	10868	4.75
FWD	1333	7.50	10000	11024	8.27
SFE	1538	6.50	10000	16380	
GUD	1124	8.89	10000	9700	8.63
NCM	706	14.15	10000	12037	17.05
TSE	1941	5.15	10000	14771	
UGL	1930	5.18	10000	18605	
FKP	3676	2.72	10000	13969	3.80
TOL	923	10.83	10000	12054	
MCC	3725	3.75	13969	27751	
ALL	1041	10.43	10868	12076	
CSM	3129	3.10	9700	12579	
MCG	1957	6.15	12037	12329	
OSH	4499	2.45	11024	13812	

Total number of trades = 5

Win–loss ratio = 14 wins to 1 loss or 93%

Final capital as 30 June 2005 = $158046 (up 58.0%)

S&P/ASX 200 index = up 21.1%

July 2005 to June 2006

Code	Number of shares	Buy price ($)	Value at purchase ($)	Value at sale/ end ($)	Sell price ($)
MCC	1326	7.54	10000	8022	6.05
CSM	2666	3.75	10000	8531	3.20
ALL	881	11.35	10000	9867	11.20
OSH	3236	3.09	10000	13268	
CTX	638	15.67	10000	10948	17.16
WOR	1275	7.84	10000	25627	
MAP	2832	3.53	10000	8836	3.12
UTB	709	14.09	10000	8650	12.20
MCG	1569	6.37	10000	9100	5.80
UGL	1072	9.32	10000	15437	
WPL	249	32.10	8022	10956	
JBM	1242	7.11	8836	8222	6.62
RIN	593	15.32	9100	9755	16.45
COH	230	37.51	8650	12565	
MBL	126	65.30	8222	7554	59.95
MTS	2132	4.00	8531	8848	4.15
RIO	149	73.00	10948	11592	
ASX	298	33.10	9867	9709	
RMD	1322	5.71	7554	8196	
AQP	486	18.17	8848	7776	16.00
TIM	2457	3.97	9755	9877	
RCD	714	10.88	7776	8818	

Total number of trades = 12

Win–loss ratio = 12 wins to 10 losses or 55%

Final capital as 30 June 2006 = $126045 (up 26.0%)

S&P/ASX 200 index = up 18.7%

July 2006 to June 2007

Code	Number of shares	Buy price ($)	Value at purchase ($)	Value at sale/ end	Sell price ($)
WOR	495	20.20	10000	8083	16.33
RCD	809	12.35	10000	8009	9.90
TIM	2444	4.09	10000	7625	3.12
RIO	128	77.95	10000	8600	67.19
ROC	2386	4.19	10000	7969	3.34
CSL	188	53.00	10000	16544	
WPL	225	44.40	10000	8237	36.61
OSH	2409	4.15	10000	8263	3.43
BHP	345	28.96	10000	8594	24.91
LEI	575	17.37	10000	23719	
UGL	535	5.35	7625	7169	13.40
AWE	2519	3.28	8263	6222	2.47
COH	156	51.50	8083	9828	63.00
DJS	2321	3.45	8009	12928	
AXA	1333	6.45	8600	10211	7.66
OST	1915	4.16	7969	12313	
MGQ	1291	6.38	8237	8676	
JST	2291	3.75	8594	10804	
FMG	717	8.67	6222	24235	
MRE	1128	6.35	7169	8212	
IPL	150	65.50	9828	11955	
PDN	1130	9.03	10211	9334	

Total number of trades = 12

Win–loss ratio = 10 wins to 12 losses or 45%

Final capital as 30 June 2007 = $138720 (up 38.7%)

S&P/ASX 200 index = up 23.7%

July 2007 to June 2008

Code	Number of shares	Buy price ($)	Value at purchase ($)	Value at sale/end ($)	Sell price ($)
FMG	287	34.80	10000	8036	28.00
IPL	126	79.14	10000	23310	
MRE	1373	7.28	10000	8924	6.50
PDN	1209	8.27	10000	9394	7.77
AQP	829	12.06	10000	13861	
LEI	238	41.90	10000	10865	45.65
BKN	909	11.00	10000	8054	8.86
WAN	729	13.70	10000	9127	12.52
SEK	1358	7.36	10000	9044	6.66
DJS	1801	5.55	10000	8465	4.70
WOR	271	34.60	9394	10840	40.00
ZFX	476	18.72	8924	7402	15.55
SDG	2226	3.61	8036	7568	3.40
OST	1298	5.70	7402	9657	
CSM	1881	4.85	9127	9292	4.94
FLT	260	30.97	8054	6279	24.15
CSL	265	34.10	9044	9460	
HVN	1762	6.15	10840	8986	5.10
ASX	146	51.50	7568	6186	42.37
NUF	429	14.63	6279	6830	
WOW	283	29.90	8465	7700	27.21

Cash on hand as at 30 June 2008 due to lack of shares available = $43029

Total number of trades = 16

Win–loss ratio = 8 wins to 13 losses or 38%

Final capital as 30 June 2008 = $106147 (up 6.1%)

S&P/ASX 200 index = down 16.9%

Note: Alan recommended holding cash from early August 2007.

July 2008 to June 2009

Code	Number of shares	Buy price ($)	Value at purchase ($)	Value at sale/end ($)	Sell price ($)
IPL	1081	9.25	10000	7308	6.76
MCC	544	18.36	10000	7877	14.48
MGX	3174	3.15	10000	8030	2.53
RIO	94	105.69	10000	8815	93.78
CSL	281	35.58	10000	10082	35.88
STO	552	18.10	10000	6216	11.26
WSA	1020	9.80	10000	8772	8.60
AQP	718	13.91	10000	8688	12.10
OSH	1709	5.85	10000	5983	3.50

No positions were held at the end of the period because there were no shares appearing on the list from late October 2008 onwards.

Total number of trades = 9

Win–loss ratio = 1 win to 8 losses or 11%

Final capital as 30 June 2009 = $81771 (down 18.2%)

S&P/ASX 200 index = down 24.2%

Note: Alan recommended holding cash for the entire period.

July 2009 to June 2010

Code	Number of shares	Buy price ($)	Value at purchase ($)	Value at sale/end ($)	Sell price ($)
KCN	1074	9.31	10000	9129	8.50
KCN	1118	8.94	10000	10587	
GUD	1044	9.57	10000	8665	8.30
CPU	793	12.60	10000	8604	10.85
JBH	487	20.51	10000	9014	18.51
BHP	229	43.48	10000	8718	38.07
WHC	1838	5.44	10000	8197	4.46
SMX	1481	6.75	10000	7760	5.24

Code	Number of shares	Buy price ($)	Value at purchase ($)	Value at sale/end ($)	Sell price ($)
MRM	3571	2.80	10000	8749	2.45
CBA	175	56.90	10000	8855	50.60
IRE	1206	8.29	9129	10480	
FLT	482	18.06	8718	7808	16.20
SEK	1230	7.04	8665	8622	
IFL	1489	6.05	9014	8919	
ORI	325	25.09	8197	8190	
NWS	485	18.01	8749	8124	16.75
TRS	503	15.50	7808	7897	

Total number of trades = 11

Win–loss ratio = 4 wins to 17 losses or 19%

Final capital as 30/6/08 = $88103 (down 11.9%)

S&P/ASX 200 index = up 8.8%

Note: Alan recommended cash and an alternative list of shares during July–August 2009, which returned an average of 6.7%.

July 2010 to June 2011

Code	Number of shares	Buy price ($)	Value at purchase ($)	Value at sale/end ($)	Sell price ($)
BKN	1400	7.14	10000	10850	7.75
SEK	1420	7.04	10000	10153	7.15
IFL	1623	6.16	10000	11523	7.10
KCN	1043	9.58	10000	9669	9.27
FWD	1089	9.18	10000	12088	11.10
ORI	407	24.55	10000	10175	25.00
WES	355	28.09	10000	10575	29.79
TRS	636	15.70	10000	11321	17.80

(continued)

July 2010 to June 2011 (*cont'd*)

Code	Number of shares	Buy price ($)	Value at purchase ($)	Value at sale/ end ($)	Sell price ($)
IRE	1170	8.54	10000	9606	8.21
RHC	722	13.84	10000	12974	
CMJ	3368	3.14	10575	11114	3.30
RIV	1037	9.26	9606	16799	
CEY	1690	6.02	10175	10410	6.16
HDF	7861	1.44	11321	12420	
ANN	830	13.39	11114	11603	13.98
AVO	2836	3.58	10153	8678	3.06
PRU	3358	3.10	10410	9067	2.70
SFR	1352	7.15	9669	8518	6.30
ILU	1019	8.51	8678	16834	
IGO	1516	7.65	11603	9339	6.16
LNC	4141	2.62	10850	11802	
MML	1339	6.36	8518	8663	6.47
BLY	2147	4.35	9339	8738	
AGO	3302	3.66	12088	12449	
MIN	989	11.64	11523	11413	
MND	470	19.25	9067	8719	
CQO	2489	3.48	8663	8512	

Total number of trades = 17

Win–loss ratio = 17 wins to 10 losses or 63%

Final capital as 30/June 2011 = $120,660 (up 20.7%)

S&P/ASX 200 index = up 7.1%

Note: Alan's recommendations would have returned 6.1%.

Cumulative performance comparison

Date	S&P/ASX 200 index		Blue Chip Report	
July 2001		$100 000		$100 000
2001/2002	−7.90%	$92 100	7.60%	$107 600
2002/2003	−5.80%	$86 758	11.30%	$119 759
2003/2004	16.80%	$101 333	48.60%	$177 962
2004/2005	21.10%	$122 714	58.00%	$281 180
2005/2006	18.70%	$145 662	26.00%	$354 287
2006/2007	23.70%	$180 184	38.70%	$491 396
2007/2008	−16.90%	$147 931	6.10%	$521 371
2008/2009	−24.20%	$112 132	−18.20%	$426 481
2009/2010	8.80%	$122 000	−11.90%	$375 730
2010/2011	7.10%	$130 662	20.70%	$453 506

Please note the following:

- These results do not include external costs such as taxation, and so on.

- Past performance is no guarantee of future returns.

- This simulation is a guide only and has not been independently audited.

Recommended further reading

The only totally risk-free investment I know of is knowledge

Active Investing by Alan Hull (Wrightbooks, 2009)

Buffettology by Mary Buffett (Simon & Schuster, 1997)

Greatest Investing Stories by Richard Phalon (John Wiley & Sons, 2001)

The Bear Book by John Rothchild (John Wiley & Sons, 1998)

The Great Crash by John Kenneth Galbraith (Penguin Books, 1954)

Top Stocks series by Martin Roth (Wrightbooks, annual)

Trade My Way by Alan Hull (Wrightbooks, 2011)

Index

The Blue Chip Report
subscription form

*** Includes the ActVest Newsletter ***

Please print all details clearly, tick where appropriate, sign, date and fax or post to:

ActVest P/L 53 Grange Drive Lysterfield Victoria, 3156.
or Fax 03 9778 7062

Please forward your enquiries to enquiries@alanhull.com

YES □ I wish to subscribe to *The Blue Chip Report* at $99 per month, plus the joining fee of $49.50 AND receive as a bonus, the ActVest Trade Recorder FREE (valued at $49.50).

OR

YES □ I wish to subscribe to *The Blue Chip Report* at $990 per annum, plus the joining fee of $49.50 AND receive as a bonus, the ActVest Trade Recorder FREE (valued at $49.50).

Please charge to my Credit Card: VISA □   MasterCard   □

Card No._____ Expiry ____ / ____

My full Name _____

E-mail address_____

Daytime Phone_____

Please sign here _____ Dated:__/__/__

Please read the conditions explained overleaf as signing this form indicates your acceptance of these terms.

General Conditions of Subscription

Support   Support is provided via email and is strictly limited to products supplied by ActVest Pty. Ltd. This support specifically does not include financial advice of any kind.

Back Issues   Forwarding of back issues will attract an administrative surcharge.

Liability   Whilst all care has been taken, Alan Hull and his servants and/or agents accept no liability for any reliance upon any material and information provided by them and no responsibility is accepted for any losses, charges, damages or expenses which may be sustained or incurred by any participant or otherwise by reason of any reliance upon the materials or information given.

Cancellation   Subscriptions must be cancelled in writing.

Suspension   There is no suspension facility provided for either monthly or annual subscriptions.

Tax Invoice   Tax invoices will be issued on an annual basis.

Conditions for Monthly Subscription

Billing Details ActVest Pty. Ltd. ABN-44 101 040 939 must retain customer credit card details for the purpose of billing $99 on the first day of each month.

Cancellation   Monthly subscriptions will be terminated at the end of the current monthly billing period.

Conditions for Annual Subscription

Cancellation   Annual subscriptions that are cancelled mid-term will be refunded on a pro-rata basis, less a $99 administration fee.

Acknowledgement

- I, the undersigned, acknowledge that I have read and understand the above advice and disclaimer.

- I acknowledge that I will at all times in the future indemnify Alan Hull and his servants and/or agents against all actions, liabilities, proceedings, claims, costs and expenses which I may suffer, incur, or sustain in connection with, or arising in any way whatsoever in reliance upon any material, information or opinions provided by Alan Hull and his servants and/or agents.

- I acknowledge that any future dealings I may undertake in any securities will be entered into freely and voluntarily and without inducement or encouragement from Alan Hull and his servants and/or agents.

Martin Roth's *Top Stocks*—published in November every year.

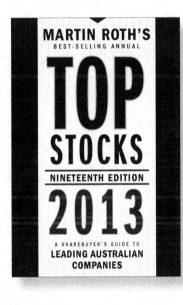 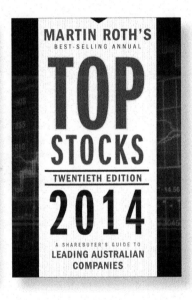

Available in print and e-book formats

Printed in Australia
03 Feb 2020
130029

Printed in Australia
03 Feb 2020
730229